SEVEN STEPS

TO A FIRM FOUNDATION IN YESHUA

SEVEN STEPS
TO A FIRM FOUNDATION IN YESHUA

Dr. Yossie Meir

Meir, Yossie, *Seven Steps to a Firm Foundation in Yeshua*
© 2015 by Ariel Ministries

ISBN: 978-1-935174-50-9

Library of Congress Control Number:
2015933198

REL101000 RELIGION / Messianic Judaism

All rights reserved. No part of this publication may be reproduced, distributed, or transmitted in any form or by any means, including photocopying, recording, or other electronic or mechanical methods, without the prior written permission of the publisher, except in the case of brief quotations embodied in critical reviews and certain other noncommercial uses permitted by copyright law. For permission requests, write to the publisher at the address below.

Different Scripture versions were used throughout this book. A note at the end of each verse indicates the source. All translations are public domain and were found on BibleGateway.com.

Editor: Christiane Jurik, M.A.
Copy-Editor: Sue Kennedy
Printed in the United States of America
Cover illustration by Jesse and Josh Gonzales (*http://www.vipgraphics.net*)

Published by Ariel Ministries
P.O. Box 792507
San Antonio, TX 78279-2507
www.ariel.org

Special thanks to

Dr. Robert M. Lewis

and his outstanding booklet "1 to 1."

Contents

INTRODUCTION 1

STEP 1
THE BIBLE 9
    Revelation 12
    Inspiration 14
    Prophecy 14
    Things to think about 17

STEP 2
THE CHARACTER OF GOD 23
    Truth 25
    Justice 26
    Grace 27
    Love 28
    Immutable 29
    Omniscient 30
    Omnipotent 31
    Omnipresent 31
    Holy 32
    Things to think about 33

STEP 3
YESHUA—THE GOD-MAN OF HISTORY 37
    Things to think about 51

STEP 4
SIN 55
- *Things to think about* 65

STEP 5
JUSTIFICATION AND SANCTIFICATION– THE CONFUSION OF IT ALL 67
- *Things to think about* 73

STEP 6
LIVING IN THE POWER OF THE HOLY SPIRIT 77
- *Things to think about* 86

STEP 7
A BALANCED LIFE IN YESHUA 89
- *Things to think about* 99

POSTSCRIPT 103
ABOUT THE AUTHOR 105

Foreword

By Dr. Arnold Fruchtenbaum

Ariel Ministries exists in order to share the Gospel with Jewish people and to disciple Jewish and Gentiles believers through intensive Bible teaching from a Jewish perspective. This goal has been the driving force of all publishing work Ariel Ministries has ever performed, and the reason why we have decided to publish this work is because we are convinced it will fulfill our purposes. *Seven Steps to a Firm Foundation in Yeshua* can be used to equip new Jewish and Gentile believers with a solid foundation of their faith.

In II Timothy 3:16-17, God, too, expresses a goal when He says:

[16] Every scripture inspired of God is also profitable for teaching, for reproof, for correction, for instruction which is in righteousness. [17] That the man of God may be complete, furnished completely unto every good work.

God clearly states that the goal of His Word is to make *the man of God complete*. His Word is to grow the believer into a person whose spiritual maturity manifests itself in his practical ability to perform *every good work*.

My friend, Dr. Yossie Meir, has successfully provided a book, which helps the young believer to use Scripture in the God-ordained way: to teach, to reproof, to correct, and to instruct him in righteousness. By consistently combining doctrine with practical exercises, Dr. Meir offers a great teaching tool for mentors and small group Bible study leaders alike. Rather than forcing his own opinions on the new believer, he encourages him to think and reason for himself. The seven steps he challenges him to take examine such fundamental questions as, "What is the Bible?", "Can we understand the character of God?", "Who is Yeshua?", "What is sin?", "What happens at salvation?", "How do we live in the power of the Holy Spirit?", and "How do we live a balanced life in Yeshua?"

Upon completing this Bible study, the reader will have a firm foundation for his faith. From it, he will be able to grow in maturity and become a useful and faithful servant of the living God.

Introduction

Christianity has long suffered by its own hands and also from the hands of its enemies. A generation ago, in the South, it was not uncommon to go into a café early in the morning and find a man or a woman quietly explaining the Gospel of *Yeshua* (Hebrew for Jesus) to another person. Things have changed. Sharing Messiah with people is much more abnormal outside the walls of a church building and even is becoming uncommon in those venues. Why the changed environment? There are several reasons, but one significant factor is that believers seem increasingly inclined to have a spiritual experience and less inclined to share the gospel message of Yeshua with someone else. A second reason is that Bible literacy is dramatically diminished in this modern day.

    Within these pages are simple, yet timeless truths. For adequate discipleship, it is essential to establish the Bible as being *completely* true, always relevant, and written entirely from the hand of Almighty God. Those certainties are foundation stones for any good study of the Bible. If a person doubts the presence of God throughout the pages of Scripture, then it does not make much sense to try to explain things about the *character* of God to him. If a person does not understand the character of God, then the idea of Yeshua, the only God-Man of human history, will make no sense. If anyone doubts Yeshua's life and finished work on the cross, then neither will he see himself as a sinner in need of salvation. See the flow? If one does not believe his own sin, then Yeshua's work will never quite click with him. Obviously, one important passage in Scripture follows another.

If the Bible is not real, then there is no divine requirement to live a Spirit-filled life in this world. Scripture will become only another lofty idea, just an empty philosophy on the often winding road of life. It is crucial for a person to become convinced of the authenticity of Scripture, the inerrancy of the entire Bible, and view it for what it is: God's inspired written account of the major events of history and His plan of salvation, freely extended for humanity to know. If one does not have that assurance, he may grasp any alternative philosophy, though he will only take hold of a vacuous one. Having assurance about the divine inspiration of all Scripture does not mean that your Bible translation does not have a few typos or grammatical mistakes. There may be differences in a few words in the various translations, some of which are more accurate than others. However, know that those differences do not change the context of what God tells us about a matter; neither does having other translations affect Bible stories. Thus, the text itself is true, protected from error by the Holy Spirit of God. All events described in the Scriptures really happened; not one is a fabrication!

The Bible mentions a period called the Millennium. Theologians and scholars may hold differing views about that time span. Some adhere to a pre-millennial view. They teach that Messiah will come back to establish His kingdom on earth before the thousand years begin during which He will reign in Jerusalem. Others hold to a post-millennial view, an amillennial view, or a "Millennium is now" view. The point: just because there are differing views about the precise beginning of the Millennium does not mean that someday there is not going to be such a time period as a Millennium like the Bible assures us.

The book you hold in your hands does not guess at uncertain times within the Bible. It will not try to pinpoint the exact day of the Second Coming of Yeshua or of the rapture of the Church. These events, although certainties to happen, are left for believers in Yeshua to understand as being true. The precise times, on the other hand, cannot be known to us. Neither will certain other events of Bible history be known to us in their entirety—historical events, like the biographic history of Melchizedek or the precise locations of the pre-Temple lodging places of the Ark of the Covenant. Rather than trying to deliver yet another argument for or against certain exact dates, this book presents seven fundamental steps one must grasp as he seeks a proper understanding of God. This author views the principles herein as essential to having a more complete view of of the invisible God and His matchless plan for our abundant life in Yeshua. For us to follow God, we must understand that foremost, He wants each of us to become mature in Yeshua.

In this day, it is important for us to firmly plant both feet on the fertile ground of Yeshua *Ha'Mashiach* (Hebrew for Messiah). Some may use diet, meditation, soft music, phone text, or other things in order to manage their day. Though some of these may be useful at times, none of them will work for holding a proper relationship with the living God. Only a correct understanding of Scripture, leading to a right relationship with God, will ever bring lasting satisfaction to us. Anything else may seem right for a time but will leave a person empty and ultimately in the vernacular "howling at the moon."

Doubtlessly, the biggest error in the Christian community today is the notion that the Jew is no longer important in God's overall design. However, as we will see, the Jew has always had a crucial role in God's plan for humanity—past, present, and future. Israel as a people has been selected from the sea of humanity to be essential. This is not so because the Jew is more special than the Gentile, but because God made a promise to Abraham, Isaac, and Jacob (Genesis 12), saying that, through them, He would bring forgiveness to the entire human race. In addition, God exclusively chose Jewish men to write down both the Old and the New Testaments.

The fact that 4,000 years have passed since Abraham lived, yet the Jew is numerically the same today as he was in antiquity, is not merely blind luck. Over the same time period, every culture, as it existed in ancient times, has ceased: the Jebusites, the Horites, the Hivites, the Canaanites, the Egyptians, the Scythians, the Babylonians, the Medes, the Persians, the Greeks, the Romans, the many hordes of central Asian tribes that overran Europe about 1,500 years ago, and many more groups no longer hold to their original cultures and, in most cases, have died out. Today, the Jew alone continues to exist, much as he did 2,500 years ago, a sign from above that proclaims to an ever-watchful world, "God keeps His promises!"

The fact that, today, the Jew is often excluded from consideration in the universal church is a curiosity. This peculiarity has much to do with certain wrong teachings in many denominations, especially some large European churches. This wrong thinking, being a culmination of certain humanistic doctrines of various theologians, historians, philosophers, and scientists, is becoming larger. What these people have written or said is often a continuation of the same error that many of the writers of the New Testament addressed so well in their books. Nevertheless, because of a lengthy period of teaching contempt for the Jew, certain churches have persecuted this group of people, even killed many, culminating in the worst expression of anti-Semitism, the *Shoah* (Hebrew for Holocaust). Here is the actual truth: God loves the Jew, so Satan hates him! That is the long and short of it. The Shoah is nothing more than an accumulation of Satan's long-time war against the Creator of heaven and earth. Thus, the survival of the Jew, often amidst great persecution, is a sign that when God says "forever," He means forever! It is critical that the world understand that truth.

In a review of Hollywood legends, old and recent, many stories reveal broken lives, demonstrative of striving for the brass ring of a moment in time that the world may hold dear, rather than the pursuit to understand the only God-Man of human history. Throughout the centuries, famous as well as ordinary people have tried to find peace through fame, money, divorce, alcoholism, hedonism, multiple marriages, and every manner of indiscretion. Life does not simply work itself out when a person chases the fickle longings of the world. What we wrestle to hold onto, in reality, is a mirage; it is "smoke and mirrors;" it is like grasping the wind in your hand. When we grab for anything other than God, it vanishes in our hands and becomes nothing at all.

In the following pages are seven fundamental steps to a strong foundation in Yeshua, steps that can lead one to a full life with

God, satisfaction, and onward to life everlasting. Eternity is its own reward, and it awaits you! The Scriptures are the ideal way to learn about God, exactly who He is, and His amazing revelation of Himself over the ages. If you do not own a Bible, there are several very good ones available for continuing this study. This author recommends the New American Standard Bible, the New King James Version, or the English Standard Version. The American Standard Bible of 1901 is excellent, but it has no commentary. There are other good Bible translations, but some are watered down and very poorly written. Please be careful which Bible you choose. As for commentaries, we would like to make you aware of Dr. Arnold Fruchtenbaum's work, for he has thoroughly investigated the Scriptures from a Messianic Jewish perspective. Other commentators are Alfred Edersheim, Charles C. Ryrie, and J. Dwight Pentecost.

To develop a solid foundation and understanding of God's Word, it is suggested that you work on a chapter of this booklet per week. Preferably, you should be able to find a period when you can commit to eight consecutive weeks of study. Each lesson requires about two hours a week for you and your teacher. We might advise you not to hurriedly read through the lessons or to complete a lesson at the last minute before a meeting. If God went through the trouble of writing you His words so that you may be a beneficiary of what the Bible says, you too can invest the appropriate time to study what was written about an important subject. Write your answers in pencil. When you meet with your leader, you may want to rethink some of what you have previously written. That is fine. It is normal to do that. Please remember to pray before each lesson. Pray that God will show you the true meaning of what He has written for you to know.

Study Tips in a Nutshell

1. Work with a leader.

2. Use a pencil because it is normal to erase a lot, especially at first.

3. It does not matter which translation of the Bible you use, but you should strive to use the same translation as your leader in this study. We recommend the NASB, the ESV, the NKJV, or the ASV.

4. Be rested when you study the Word of God each day.

5. Do not try to rush through all the Scriptures of this book at the last minute. It is better to cancel a lesson than to hurry through the material.

6. Try not to cancel a lesson at the last minute.

Blessings to you in your quest to more fully understand God's Word!

Step 1

The Bible

This lesson may be the most important truth in your life. How do you know with all certainty that the Bible is God's Word, that it is inerrant, that it was written by the Holy Spirit, and that it is the *only* Word of God? Almost everyone has an opinion about the Bible. Some think it to be a brilliant treatise composed by well-meaning writers from antiquity. Others say it is a collection of wise writings by various gifted authors. Again others may say that God only wrote portions of the Bible. And then there are the many who do not believe the Bible is the Word of God at all.

What you think about the Bible most likely proclaims many things about your life. If you do not believe it to be written by God, then your life probably shows it. If you do feel it was written by God and is relevant today, your life is likely much more hopeful, filled with the light of future eternity.

It is safe to say that many people do not feel the Bible to be relevant to their lives today. Others hold to the Bible's every word, so much so, they may worship the book as if it was God or bludgeon others who do not read the Bible with endless verses. This practice can be an example of spiritual pride. The Bible may seem random or chaotic to some people, but it really is not either. Which is it then? Is the Bible true, partially true, or not true at all? The salient question is if we can say with all certainty that the Bible is God's only written statement to man. A second, less urgent question to consider is: Can the Bible only be understood by those who recite passages to others in endless repetition?

The Bible as a whole was written over a period of about 1,600 years. The Spirit of God placed both parts of the book in the hands of faithful men, and according to their personalities, they wrote what God wanted them to write. The Bible is a collection of 66 books, 39 of which are found in the Old Testament and 27 in the New Testament. The Bible's forty authors held several different vocations. They were shepherds, princes, poets, farmers, fishermen, nobility, and ordinary people like you and me. They expressed a single, central story: "We are all sinners in desperate need of a Savior."

In college, certain writings of antiquity are confidently taught as historic fact. Today, libraries throughout the world are overflowing with books written by such men as Julius Caesar (*History of the Gallic Wars*), Herodotus, Homer, Hippocrates, and many others. The large gaps of time between when each man wrote his manuscript and when others made copies of these writings are remarkable. All we have today are the copies, and these copies were made 800 or 1,000 years after the death of the authors. Still, the texts are taken at face value and considered equal to the originals.

Not so the Bible. Its origin and validity are often at the center of scrutinizing studies of historians, theologians, and scientists who try hard to disprove it. When the Dead Sea Scrolls were discovered, they confirmed the accuracy of the ancient texts:

> The Dead Sea Scrolls are a collection of 972 texts discovered between 1946 and 1956 at Khirbet Qumran in the West Bank. They were found in caves about a mile inland from the northwest shore of the Dead Sea, from which they derive their name. The texts are of great historical, religious, and linguistic significance because they include the earliest known surviving manuscripts of works later included in the Hebrew Bible canon, along with extra-biblical manuscripts which preserve evidence of the diversity of religious thought in late Second Temple Judaism.[1]

For several years, the discovery of the Dead Sea Scrolls yielded multiple copies of Old Testament books, some written a few hundred years before Yeshua walked the earth, as well as some non-canonical books. Some of these books were only written a few hundred years after the original writings, called autographs. Did you know that we have copies of the New Testament today that date to the year A.D. 125? There are no other writings of antiquity whose date of origin and the date of the first copies lie that close together. Remember: Why would God write something for us to see and then leave it to chance whether or not we discover it?

---

[1] Greer, Thomas H., *A Brief History of the Western World*. Published as "Just the Facts101" by Cram101 Publishing, 2013, as e-book.

The Scriptures do not claim to be philosophical works for the improvement of mankind nor some lofty ideal that enables us to be properly informed. No, this wise, supernatural book is the actual dictate of our living God, freely given to us to lift us out of often desperate lives. We read this in 2 Timothy 3:16 where it says:

> *All scripture is given by inspiration of God, and is profitable for doctrine, for reproof, for correction, for instruction in righteousness.* (NKJV)

We may dispute its words, as many seem to want to do, but if we trust its authority, the Bible will greatly improve our lives on earth.

More importantly, the Bible provides us a magnification of life, although of everlasting life. When we accept the Bible's divine authorship, if we honestly look to Yeshua for our salvation, He will give us eternal life and give it to us for free! That's a pretty good trade!

There are three important principles a book has to fulfill to qualify as the very Word of God: revelation, inspiration, and authentication.

Revelation

Try as we may, if God had not revealed information about His exact nature, His unique character, His great plan of the ages, mankind would have never discovered Him through human merit alone. Mankind may use a telescope or a microscope, yet the *secret things belong to the* L<small>ORD</small> *our God, but the things revealed belong to us and to our sons forever...* (Deut. 29:29, NASB).

The authors of the Bible were free to use their own writing styles. While the prince of prophets, Isaiah, wrote in elaborate

Hebrew poetry and mentioned God over 80 times, the narrative of the Book of Esther surprises with the complete absence of any explicit reference to God, worship, prayer, or sacrifice. The contrast could not be bigger. Nevertheless, God superintended every word of the Bible so that the final passages are inerrant. Thus, God revealed Himself in that way to us, otherwise, we would not know too much about Him.

There are people who were born blind or deaf or rendered that way by a tragedy, who came to knowledge of God through their other senses. But there is no contradiction with the other senses! The circular cycle of nature, the growth of mankind, the dying and new life of once dead looking tree branches more than shout that there is a God and that He is not silent. Romans 1:20 says:

> *For since the creation of the world His invisible attributes, His eternal power and divine nature, have been clearly seen, being understood through what has been made, so that they are without excuse.* (NASB)

Though by general revelation the idea of the existence of God is understood by all followers of Yeshua, we would not really know His design of the world, His plan for mankind, unless He informed us and told us about the story of humanity and about Himself. His written word is certain. When God tells us that life began in a garden, that life came into being by His breath, that existence, as we know it, was not in place until Adam and Eve lived, we can be sure that He speaks the truth in Psalm 33:9:

> *He spoke and it came to be; He commanded, and it stood firm.* (ESV)

Inspiration

The English word *inspiration* is derived from the Greek word *theopneustos* from which we get the English word *pneumonia*. *Theopneustos* literally means "God breathed." Notice that *theopneustos* does not merely mean a passionate emotion, as the word may commonly be used today. We already looked at 2 Timothy 3:16 and learned that *All Scripture is inspired by God.*

Romans 15:4 adds this thought:

For whatever was written in former days was written for our instruction, that through endurance and through the encouragement of the Scriptures we might have hope. (ESV)

This verse lets us know that the Scriptures were written in order to inform us, not to ask our permission; so the words of Scripture are much more meaningful than a mere attractive collection of passionate writings.

Prophecy

In the Bible, prophecy is not intended to be a mystical, personal experience, as many may believe. Prophecy is intended to authenticate the words of Scripture, so that we can know that all Scripture comes directly from the mind of God, not from the mind of man. Old Testament prophecies were written between 500 and 1,500 years prior to the life of Yeshua, and some were revealed a few thousand years before His birth. The Bible is largely prophecy, a great amount having already occurred. All prophecy precisely predicts Yeshua's life and public ministry on this earth 2,000 years ago.

One of the most obvious prophecies is found in the Book of Isaiah. These words were written about 700 years before the birth of Yeshua. That would be like going back in time to before the life of Christopher Columbus. Jewish believers in Yeshua point to Isaiah—especially chapter 53—for a prediction of God's provision of a **vicarious atonement** for all sinners, in other words, the atonement through Yeshua. To fully appreciate what the Prophet Isaiah is saying, start at Isaiah 52:14 and read through the entire chapter 53. Over the centuries, these verses have convinced many men (including some rabbis) and women, Jewish and Gentile, to worship only Yeshua as God's Messiah. Isaiah 52:14 says this about Him:

> *As many were astonished at you— his appearance was so marred, beyond human semblance, and his form beyond that of the children of mankind—* (ESV)

Isaiah 53:3 adds:

> *He was despised and rejected by men; a man of sorrows, and acquainted with grief; and as one from whom men hide their faces he was despised, and we esteemed him not.* (ESV)

And in Isaiah 53:5, we finally read:

> *But He was pierced through for our transgressions, He was crushed for our iniquities; The chastening for our well-being fell upon Him, And by His scourging we are healed.* (NASB)

Now read the first part of Psalm 22. These verses predict the crucifixion of Yeshua, accurately recorded some 1,000 years before His unique birth on earth. Write down verse 15 in the lines below:

_____
_____
_____

Another verse which predicts the First Coming of Messiah (*Shiloh*) is found in Genesis 49:10:

> *The scepter shall not depart from Judah, Nor the ruler's staff from between his feet, Until Shiloh comes, And to him shall be the obedience of the peoples.* (NASB)

From the time the above prophecy was given until Yeshua's birth, the tribe of Judah kept its identity, often despite difficult times.

> *But as for you, Bethlehem Ephrathah, who are too little to be among the clans of Judah, from you shall come forth for Me one who is to be ruler in Israel, whose coming forth is from old, from ancient days.* (Micah 5:2, ESV)

This verse is an early predictive declaration of the birth city of the Messiah, Bethlehem Ephrathah, the city of David. In Hebrew, Bethlehem means "house of bread." Translated, Ephrathah means "fruit from the vine." The very name of the birthplace of Yeshua is also a picture of the believer's future communion with Him celebrated in churches around the world.

As to the miraculous circumstance of the birth itself, we read in Isaiah 7:14:

> *The Lord Himself will give you a sign. Behold, a virgin shall be with child and shall call His name, Emmanuel* (sic God with us, ESV).

Seven hundred fifty years before Yeshua, the Prophet Isaiah predicted that He would be born from the womb of a virgin.

There are many other Old Testament prophecies about Yeshua that came to pass exactly as they were written. Several hundred chapters or verses were predictive of the Yeshua's future public ministry. Can you think of any other event that moved from prediction to historic fact? People calling themselves mystics might have had a few close calls, but they are like blindfolded men pinning a tail on a donkey while they are in the basement and the donkey is in the attic.

Things to think about

There is no other document in the world that has predictive historical accuracy as is seen in the Bible that sits on your table! Fulfilled Scripture establishes the Bible to be a **trustworthy** document for people to learn about the mind of God.

There might be differences in the pages of various versions of Scripture, but that does not mean the Bible is not utterly true. It only means that language has changed, a copier may have made a minor mistake, or a translator may have taken a bit more freedom than others. God has protected the **integrity** of everything He talks about in the Bible, so that Bibles today perfectly communicate the very mind of God.

There are some books of antiquity, such as the Apocrypha or the pseudoepigraphic writings, which may hold some **historical accuracy.** Nevertheless, neither the Bible-copying Masoretic Jewish scribes nor the majority of Jewish scholars nor the leaders of the early church considered them to be Scriptures. The reason: these books were written to influence people into a Greek culture, a process called **Hellenization**. They were not written to reflect the life of Yeshua. Often, "extra-biblical" books tell interesting stories, some true, some partially true, but they do not reveal the actual character of God, as do the 66 books of the inspired Bible.

Within the Bible, there are many prophecies about the public life of Yeshua. For some people, these fulfilled prophecies are not enough! No amount of fulfilled prophecies would be enough to satisfy curiosity if there is no faith that God is exactly who He says

He is. The Bible contains true truth and is not merely another "helpful symbolic" philosophy. Fulfilled prophecy is sufficient proof in human history that Yeshua is the only God-Man who came down to earth and discipled 12 simple, uneducated men—men who would, someday, change the world.

Today, the Word of God can be found everywhere on the planet, in just about every translation. Many homes even have it in various printings. The Bible provides clear explanations about God for countless peoples living on the earth, both now and in past centuries. The Bible has continued to exist despite incredible persecution, war, prohibition, restriction, sanctions, censorship, and fire. These days, much of the world appears to have given up on the idea of destroying the Bible. In fact, the opposite seems to be happening, in that the planet is flooded with endless commentaries about the meaning of the Bible and some translations that may significantly dilute God's Word.

Notice, too, that when a person reads the Word of God, his free will (volition) may cause him to rearrange or change what God has to say on a subject. Thomas Jefferson's Bible is a good example of that practice. He did not especially like the word sin, so he clipped it out of his Bible whenever he found it. Any diversion from the partnership between God giving us truth and man receiving truth can result in wrong interpretations of Scripture. However, in a continuum that begins in the mind of the Trinity to later become visible in the thoughts and actions of men, God has given us a perfect book that is inerrant.

The following is a look at the right process for understanding the Bible:

- ➤ **Revelation:** Scripture revealed by God.
- ➤ **Inspiration:** Authors were inspired by God.
- ➤ **Transcription and replication:** Men copied and recopied Scripture.
- ➤ **Translation:** Men translated Scripture into other languages. Here is an even greater opportunity for corruption of God's Word. Confusion may follow.
- ➤ **Preaching:** Scripture is proclaimed to others.
- ➤ **Illumination:** The Holy Spirit illuminates the believer when he hears and reads the Word of God.
- ➤ **Application:** what a person does with the Scripture he hears.

Notice that God took the initiative to perfectly record His Word to us in the pages of Scripture. From the outset, through "revelation" and "inspiration," God insured there was no error about what He said; there is no final conflict. There are other doors for errors to creep in though. When man transcribed the Word, he had to pay special attention not to drop a word or take out a whole passage. Translations are an even bigger opportunity for error. But the biggest one is when the Bible is preached and taught. The dependency on the person interpreting the Word is huge. Yet, you must know that His written Word to us is perfect. When you read this unique book, you will understand that it is completely true; it is not just another passionate manifesto.

Thus, it is important that you hear the Word of God from the mouth of a godly man, not just from a good talker. The latter may speak some truth, but if his heart is unbelieving, if he is misled himself, he can only mislead others.

Is it possible that God would record His Bible perfectly, then let His words be distorted through the vain philosophies of man? Be faithful to let the Scriptures fill your heart. If a passage does not make sense to you or if it seems to contradict modern philosophies and scientific theories, pray that God may reveal His truth to you over time and help you understand. Don't seek to contend with others what God has written to you. Begin to interact with what He has written you. You will not be disappointed!

1. In your own words, summarize 2 Timothy 3:15-17.

_____
_____
_____
_____
_____
_____

2. List the right process of how to understand the Bible.

_____
_____
_____
_____
_____
_____
_____
_____
_____

3. What will you do from now on if you come to a passage that's difficult to understand?

_____

_____

4. According to John 5:39, what is the main reason to study the Bible?

_____

_____

5. Some people are willing to take the words of Yeshua literally, but not other parts of the Scriptures. According to John 5:46-47, why is this inconsistent thinking?

_____

_____

_____

_____

6. In John 14:6 and 17:17, what does Yeshua say about truth?

_____

_____

_____

_____

7. Memorize 2 Timothy 3:16.

Seven Steps to a Firm Foundation in Yeshua

Step 2

The Character of God

If God is someone who we would worship, He has to possess unassailable character. His character traits are known as His **attributes**. Scripture teaches us there was never a time when God did not have the attributes we are going to discuss in this chapter. God possesses all of them, not merely some of them. The nature of God is indescribably different than the nature of man. To know Him, or more importantly, for Him to know us, we must first understand that He is **perfect**. He was always perfect, and He will always be perfect throughout eternity.

In this life, no mere human is completely perfect, so this attribute of God may be difficult to understand. No imperfection is a part of His being, not even a small one. In the historical books of the Old Testament, we see God constantly moving among mankind, placing His unique stamp on every outcome of human behavior. No person is ever able to be other than himself; neither will God ever be anyone other than Himself.

The Bible tells us that God was known to Moses as YHVH (*Yahweh*):

> *Then Moses said to God, "Behold, I am going to the sons of Israel, and I will say to them, 'The God of your fathers has sent me to you.' Now they may say to me, 'What is His name?' What shall I say to them?"* (Exodus 3:13, NIV)

God's sole response to Moses' question was, "I AM!" With those two words, God proclaimed a revelatory truth to all men: He is the eternal, pre-eminent, self-existent, almighty God of time and space. There never has been nor will there ever be a time when He does not exist.

An older man of the cloth once proudly proclaimed that he had been teaching twelve adult students a class he called "Progressive Theology" during a four-year Bible course at his church. When asked the meaning of progressive theology, he replied, "In progressive theology, we teach that God knows everything about the happenings of yesterday and those of today, but he cannot foretell the future." When asked how he arrived at that conclusion, he answered, "Do you think the world would be in this terrible shape if God was able to see into the future?"

Harold Kushner, a well-known rabbi, concluded the same thing in his popular book *When Bad Things Happen to Good People*, noting that God is sad when bad things happen to us, but He is powerless to do anything about these unfortunate events.

These comments are wrong views of God. God is the God of yesterday, today, and tomorrow. There is nothing He does not know. Not one thing! We are not immortal beings; He is. He is not anthropomorphic like us. He has created each of us to have a minor portion of the character that is part of His Being. For example, man was created by Him to be personal, rational, emotional, and volitional. When He declares in Genesis 1 that we are made in His image, it does not mean we do not have limitations. He has no limitations, but we do. He created us to have good character, but on a much lesser scale than He. We may be compared to the ancient Coliseum in Rome, now it is in ruins; once it was glorious. After the fall, man has become a glorious ruin that God will someday rebuild.

He is not the God of our fantasies, not the God of our imaginations, not the God of limited powers, and not the God who visits other cultures as often spoken of in popular mythology. He is the almighty God of heaven and earth, who loves good and does not tolerate evil.

The idea of "good" and "evil" has distinct meanings among various people groups. It has a singular meaning to God. God is more powerful than the Egyptian sun god, the Babylonian bird god, the Assyrian moon god, or the legion of other gods often associated with movements in history. Here are some important aspects of God's unique character:

Truth

Whatever God says is completely true. His Word is timeless, unchangeable, and not a matter of one's own interpretation. He knows that we struggle with real truth. Only because we struggle with truth does not mean He struggles with it. With God, there is never an asterisk in His statement, never variance from His word, neither is there an escape clause about what He says is true. Sometimes, what He describes may make us uncomfortable. Nevertheless, His truth divides good and evil. His truth is not dependent on our definition of truth. He is God! Why would He not know what is best for each of us? Does the pot know more than the potter? (Isaiah 29:16, 64:8)

In Hebrews 4:12, we read:

For the word of God is living and active and sharper than any two-edged sword, and piercing as far as the division of soul and spirit, of both joints and marrow, and able to judge the thoughts and intentions of the heart. (NASB)

Justice

The American Constitution has many laws. Like the Jewish Talmud, some of these laws are subject to the interpretations of people who hold themselves out as experts. Resolution is why we have judges. In court, murder may mean life behind bars in one state and the death sentence in another. Not so with God. With Him, a person is either innocent or guilty of wrong. God makes a clear distinction about what is proper and what is not. Mankind will be known in this life for whatever moral choice is made. Only the shed blood of Yeshua can offset the sentence we deserve for our wrong choices in life.

Before His justice becomes too burdensome for us, let us be thankful that He has given us grace through Yeshua's blood; otherwise, we would all be guilty without the possibility of a pardon. In Jeremiah 9:25, God is pretty specific:

Behold, the days are coming, declares the LORD, when I will punish all those who are circumcised merely in the flesh— (ESV)

In 2 Chronicles 19:7, we read:

Now then let the fear of the LORD be upon you; be very careful what you do, for the LORD our God will have no part in unrighteousness or partiality or the taking of a bribe. (NASB)

Grace

Grace is not merely a prayer we say at meals; it, too, is a part of the character of God. Without grace, God's justice would be every man's end, in other words, his eternal condemnation.

Some would say that grace is receiving what you do not deserve, while justice is getting what you do deserve. The late British historian, C. S. Lewis, explained in his book *God in the Dock* that, on the matter of justice, he did believe in an eye for an eye and a tooth for a tooth, as the Old Testament provides. If someone kills another person, he deserves the death penalty. Lewis even went so far as to say that not to offer the killer a death sentence is dehumanizing. Under the principle of an eye for an eye, the killer deserves to die. We may decide to forgive the crime he committed, but he will have to pay for it. Not executing a killer who deserves to die is grace.

Being perfectly just, God will judge us all. Because part of His character is grace, He always forgives a person who is truly repentant and asks Yeshua for salvation. Not only will God forgive the repentant, He also forgets the sin. Forgetting does not mean He is ignorant about a sin, but that He never remembers an indignity done. We can easily remember, but God opts not to.

Grace, then, is "unmerited favor" or "undeserved mercy." Grace has no boundaries. Everyone who is forgiven has made many mistakes in life, mistakes that are actually sins against God. In the

Mosaic Law, there is a penalty for each sin. Our sin nature makes all of us lawbreakers. Romans 5:20 settles the matter for us:

> [18] Therefore, as one trespass led to condemnation for all men, so one act of righteousness leads to justification and life for all men. [19] For as by the one man's disobedience the many were made sinners, so by the one man's obedience the many will be made righteous. [20] Now the law came in to increase the trespass, but where sin increased, grace abounded all the more, [21] so that, as sin reigned in death, grace also might reign through righteousness leading to eternal life through Jesus Christ our Lord. (Romans 5:18-21, ESV)

Without grace, we would have no hope. Thus, God provides us grace through government, in order to protect us from ourselves. Even in the most oppressive governments, there is always God's grace. One may have to look for it a little harder in certain countries. You may want to think about that for a while! It is a major point in Scripture!

Love

For some people, the most difficult concept to understand is God's love for us. Since we do not really know how to love others or ourselves, it is hard to understand how He could possibly love us the way He says He does. Our inability to comprehend His love even hinders us to appreciate His sacrificial love for us.

In the ancient Greek language, we find four words for "love." They are *éros*, a physical love; *storgē*, an affectionate feeling; *philia*, a brotherly kind of love; and *agápe*, a divine love. God has promised us that He "agapes" each of us and wants to save everyone. That is hard to understand. Agape love is sacrificial love, a love we do not come close to understanding in all its force. Only because we fail to understand it does not mean it is not existent. C. S. Lewis admitted in one of his books that when he comes to his evening prayers and asks God to forgive him for the day's life, he says, "Forgive me Lord for I was not myself today." One day, it hit him. Who he really is, is who is looking back from the mirror each morning before he puts on what he calls his game face. That is a worthy statement about the sinfulness that entangles each of us.

Even the most pleasant person among us is not very loveable. At the moment of salvation, God's love becomes more obvious to us; it begins to change our character. The "older" we get in the Lord, the better we understand our condition.

John 3:16 describes God's perfect love for His creation:

For God so loved the world, that He gave His only begotten Son, that whoever believes in Him shall not perish, but have eternal life. (NASB)

Immutable

God is the same God to us today as He was in the lives of men like Abraham, Moses, Joshua, and David. He is no different now than He was thousands of years ago, nor will He undergo any change in His character in future time. He does not **mutate** with time. With Him, there is no genetic drift that causes change in His character. Other religions may worship a god who becomes transformed over time to accommodate various cycles in climate or need or perhaps to protect a man from the ravages of a disease. God never changes, not even a little. His character remains the same in each new age. From age to age, He is perfection incarnate. Through His great plan, He has freed us from the shackles of ourselves and the crazed world in which we live. He will pry us loose from the oppressively meaningless world in which we live.

Hebrews 13:8 perfectly describes God's immutability:

Jesus, the Messiah, is the same yesterday and today and forever! (ESV)

Omniscient

God knows everything. We do not know everything, although some people may be more aware of circumstances than others. The wisest institutions of learning on this earth have vacuous holes compared to God's knowledge. There are many areas in life we still do not know anything about, yet He has always known them, all of them.

Still, we may feel too secure about some of the few things that we do know. For example, we feel that when we discover something, we also designed it. It is said that in the arrogance of our ignorance, we have confused discovery with design.

Such objects as the airfoil, the electric motor, the steam engine, the ball, the wheel, the dam, the rocket, and all other such things have always been known to Him since the beginning of time. The fact that the earth rotates around an orbit which spins around the sun, that this planet is fastened in its proper place through gravitational attraction, all the while existing in a wide expanse of dark ether, is only a small example of God's limitless knowledge. Anything that results in life is not merely another discovery by mankind, but has existed long before we discovered it:

It is he who sits above the circle of the earth, and its inhabitants are like grasshoppers; who stretches out the heavens like a curtain, and spreads them like a tent to dwell in. (Isaiah 40:22, ESV)

God is omniscient because He made everything that ever came into existence. He *made the Bear and Orion, the Pleiades and the chambers of the south* (Job 9:9, ESV).

Omnipotent

God is the ultimate source of power of all things. The fact that we can harness energy, fly jet planes, type on computers, or explode atomic bombs does not mean that we are the source of that power. We have a little power for a brief time, which indicates that God sometimes allows us use of a tiny fraction of His omnipotence. However, we have access to that limitless power only because He has granted it to us.

> *It is He who made the earth by His power, Who established the world by His wisdom; And by His understanding He has stretched out the heavens.* (Jeremiah 10:12, NASB)

Omnipresent

God is everywhere, all the time. That is hard to imagine. We do not know of anyone who can say this of himself. Comic books may invent superheroes, but they are only fabrications. Boats, space capsules, and Times Square on New Year's Eve are limited in time and space. God is not merely a "Santa Claus" who lives in one place. Unable to comprehend omnipresence, some may get tempted to create household gods the same way the people of Babylon once did. In some churches, man-made icons are objects of worship. They are considered to be holy vessels or idols worthy of adoration. People like to make things that look holy. They love to worship an object—an idol—that can be seen or touched.

Remember, God is invisible, but His work on this planet is not. During difficult times, some people cry out to these lifeless images. They need to know though that if they reject God in life, He will be far from them at their times of need.

> *Behold, as for the proud one, His soul is not right within him; But the righteous will live by his faith.* (Habakkuk 2:4, NASB)
>
> *But my righteous one shall live by faith: And if he shrink back, my soul hath no pleasure in him.* (Hebrews 10:38, ASV)

Some people may wear amulets, carve tattoos onto their bodies, or make idols in the misplaced hope that these things can help during adversity. They may roll the dice of "fortune" in life, during circumstances of sickness, health, storm, drought, and other calamities. God views our struggles as tools through which we learn about His existence. He may even provide answers to our dilemmas. If His answer is not what we would choose for ourselves, in vanity, we may reject His response to us or even reject His existence. However, God does not only exist, He is everywhere:

> *Where can I go from Your Spirit? Or where can I flee from Your presence?* (Psalm 139:7, NASB)
>
> *Surely the righteous shall give thanks to Your name; The upright shall dwell in Your presence.* (Psalm 140:13, NASB)
>
> *And He said, 'My Presence shall go with you, and I will give you rest.'* (Exodus 33:14, NASB)

Holy

This is self-explanatory! If we do not know what "holy" means, it is further evidence that we are far from sinlessness. Holiness means "having no sin." Other than God, do you know of anyone who has no sin?

> [1] In the year that King Uzziah died I saw the Lord sitting upon a throne, high and lifted up; and the train of his robe filled the temple. [2] Above him stood the seraphim. Each had six wings: with two he covered his face, and with two he covered his feet, and with two he flew. [3] And one called to another and said: "Holy, holy, holy is the LORD of hosts; the whole earth is full of his glory!" (Isaiah 6: 1-3, ESV)

Things to think about

There is no power like God's. He is very much alive, and He is not silent. The weak gods of our vivid imaginations will fail us time and again. We may worship things like finances, relationships, possessions, or recognition—they will all fall short in time. Then, when it becomes the day for every man to die, his body returns to nothing, the same as when he was born.

In the space provided below, write down the one thing that promises you security in your life. How does it compare to what God has to offer?

_____
_____
_____
_____

The saying, "When you die, the one with the most toys wins," is a fallacy. It has certainly ushered countless people through the gates of Hades. From the unknown street person to the famous, wealthy prince, anyone who places his trust in the things of this world will have nothing at the end.

The common saying, "What goes around, comes around," is an expression derived from a biblical truth. Another popular saying is, "There is no free lunch." The connotation of these expressions is a certain assurance that, in this life, the authentic justice of God will eventually find everyone. God is the author of all justice.

Try to find out if God's justice threatens you, and if so, why this might be the case.

_____
_____
_____
_____

Most of us do not have difficulties honoring our natural parents, yet we are created beings, like everything else in life is created. Here is a great mystery: Why is it difficult to worship the God who created our parents? The word "worship" means "to acknowledge the value of." It does not mean to attribute to a person or thing a value it should not have. Also, it does not mean we should give false praise or meaningless adoration to anything. When we worship God, we acknowledge who He actually is in His real character.

Remember God's makeup. Consider, too, the actual meaning of the word "character." Now write down the attributes we looked at together. Which one means the most to you and why?

_____
_____
_____

Now think about your own character. Do you notice the wide chasm of difference between God's character and yours? Instead of feeling saddened, understand that the God of creation wants to have a right relationship with you—but only on His terms. In spite of your flaws, you are very important to Him. If He wants a relationship with you, then you must matter greatly to Him.

God is spirit. We are to worship Him *alone* in spirit and truth and not through an image of what we perceive Him to be. A spirit is not intended to be seen by our flesh during this lifetime. Truth means He is not the God of our vain imaginations; rather, He is the "I AM" of all life!

Look up John 4:24 and write it down. How about memorizing it?

_____
_____
_____

In the following verses, a few of God's attributes are described. They speak about His independence and sovereignty. Which attributes do you see? Describe them in your own terms.

Genesis 1:1, John 5:26

_____
_____
_____

Exodus 3:14, Psalm 90:2, Revelation 4:8

_____
_____
_____

1 Kings 8:27

_____
_____
_____

Choose the correct answer(s):

When the Bible claims that God is holy, it means

a) He is without sin.

b) He hates sin and loves good.

c) He is distinct from the sinner.

d) All three points are correct.

Which of God's attributes is especially comforting to you?

_____
_____

Is there an attribute that causes you problems? If so, why do you think that is?

_____
_____
_____

Step 3

Yeshua—the God-Man of History

Yeshua Ha-Mashiach is the most misunderstood person in all history. In God's incredible plan to save people, He alone is payment in full for each person who repents of his sinful nature and who asks Him to be his personal Savior. Yeshua is God's provision for every salvation. He is the Lamb of God, who offered Himself unto death on a cross for your and my sin. Yeshua is the God of all who believe on His saving name. Exactly how His death on a tree saved us from our sins may be a mystery to us. But we know it did save the soul of every believer who trusts Him as Savior.

He came to earth to die on a cross for everyone who believes on His name, who seeks Him for salvation, and who is authentically repentant.

[17] For this reason the Father loves me, because I lay down my life that I may take it up again. [18] No one takes it from me, but I lay it down of my own accord. I have authority to lay it down, and I have authority

to take it up again. This charge I have received from my Father. (John 10:17-18, ESV)

By about 33 B.C., Greek culture had established itself throughout much of the civilized world. In those days, most writing was influenced by it, and the libraries only contained Greek texts. There was a Greek translation of the Hebrew Scriptures (now commonly called the Old Testament). This translation was the Septuagint, which in Latin means "seventy."

Prior to A.D. 70, there were four principle Jewish factions. The Pharisees made up the most important sect, as they controlled the synagogue system of worship. To this day, they are considered the spiritual fathers of modern Judaism and were the ones who upheld the Oral Law. The second group, the Sadducees, conducted the sacrifices of animals for worship. The third faction was an ascetic group called Essenes. Though they splintered off the sect of the Pharisees, they were disgusted by both factions and developed their own doctrine and life style. The last group, the Zealots, also broke off from the Pharisaic sect. Its members were very political. Their goal was to establish a global Jewish theocracy. Being willing to fight for it, they mostly attracted rebels. These four factions made up the prevailing Jewish culture at the time Yeshua entered the world.

While the Jews in Israel and Babylon used the Hebrew text for the Jews living in the Greek and Roman world, the Septuagint translation of the Bible was the principle holy book at the time of Yeshua. Most quotations in the New Testament came from this translation. An entry in Wikipedia summarizes the continuation of the history of the Septuagint:

> In time the LXX (sic Septuagint) became synonymous with the "Greek Old Testament", i.e. a Christian canon of writings which incorporated all the books of the Hebrew canon, along with additional texts. The Roman Catholic and Eastern Orthodox Churches include most of the books that are in the Septuagint in their canons; however, Protestant churches usually do not. After the Protestant Reformation, many Protestant Bibles began to follow the Jewish canon and exclude the additional texts, which came to be called "Apocrypha" (originally meaning "hidden" but became synonymous with "of questionable authenticity"). The Apocrypha are included under a separate heading in the King James Version of the Bible, the basis for the Revised Standard Version.[2]

After assuming world domination, the Romans built a network of roads that stretched across the developed world, from the hills of northern Europe to the vast plains of Egypt. As a result, information could travel faster. New philosophies were no longer merely provincial; they quickly spread even to the far corners of the empire.

The Jewish people practiced a *monotheistic* (single God) system of belief, different from their Babylonian, Egyptian, and eastern neighbors who worshipped various gods for such diverse issues as harvests, fair weather, and victory in war. In that melting pot, the Jewish people continued to worship the God of Abraham, Isaac,

---

[2] en.wikipedia.org/wiki/Septuagint

and Jacob. Many of them had long followed a man-made religious book, an expanding commentary on the Bible, the *Talmud*, which originated in Babylon about 500 years before Yeshua was born.

Into this cauldron of man-made religion, the Messiah was born, by most estimates between 4 and 2 B.C. during the reign of King Herod the Great. Yeshua's simple birth was natural, but His conception was the result of a mysterious union between the Holy Spirit and his mother, a virgin maiden named Miriam (Mary). The birthing process itself was unremarkable. Miriam was not sinless, as she admits in her song (Luke 1:46-49). She was a virgin Jewish girl, and she worshiped only God. Thus, she was pure in *spirit*, but she was certainly not sinless, as some may believe.

Look up Luke 2:8-12 (ESV) and fill in the blanks:

> [8] *And in the same region there were shepherds out in the field, keeping watch over their flock by night.* [9] *And an angel of the Lord appeared to them, and the glory of the Lord shone around them, and they were filled with great fear.* [10] *And the angel said to them, "Fear not, for behold, I bring you good news of great joy that will be for all the people.* [11] *For unto you is born this day in the city of David a _____, who is _____ the Lord.* [12] *And this will be a _____ for you: you will find a baby wrapped in swaddling cloths and lying in a manger."*

After His birth, magi (non-Jewish holy men) arrived from Babylon, bringing Him certain gifts. These gifts became predictive of His future stations in life: Prophet, Priest, and King. He was given gold for His kingship, frankincense for His priesthood, and an embalming substance, myrrh, for His future death.

He grew to adulthood as a typical Jewish lad. In Luke 2:41-49, we receive a glimpse of His youth:

> [41] Now his parents went to Jerusalem every year at the Feast of the Passover. [42] And when he was twelve years old, they went up according to custom. [43] And when the feast was ended, as they were returning, the boy Jesus stayed behind in Jerusalem. His parents did not know it, [44] but supposing him to be in the group they went a day's journey, but then they began to search for him among their relatives and acquaintances, [45] and when they did not find him, they returned to Jerusalem, searching for him. [46] After three days they found him in the temple, sitting among the teachers, listening to them and asking them questions. [47] And all who heard him were amazed at his understanding and his answers. [48] And when his parents saw him, they were astonished. And his mother said to him, "Son, why have you treated us so? Behold, your father and I have been searching for you in great distress." [49] And he said to them, "Why were you looking for me? Did you not know that I must be in my Father's house?" (ESV)

At about age of thirty, Yeshua began a three-year public ministry, just as the Prophet Moses had predicted 1,500 years prior to His birth:

> The LORD your God will raise up for you a prophet like me from among you, from your brothers—it is to him you shall listen. (Deut. 18:15, ESV)

From the beginning of His ministry, Yeshua chose twelve men in whom He invested His life by discipling them about the ways of God. You may notice that these were twelve uneducated, not religious, often confused, very different from each other men who, over a three-year period, underwent a transformation in godliness. How did they do that? The answer is simple: they became convinced that Yeshua was the promised Messiah. There was one man among them, Judas Iscariot, who had a sinister agenda.

The twelve men Yeshua chose as His disciples were not the powerful men of Israel. They were ordinary fellows, who became more mature over time as a direct result of the Messiah's ministry in their lives. During the first twelve chapters of the Gospel of Matthew, Yeshua performed multiple miracles to demonstrate that He was the promised Messiah of Israel, as well as of the whole world. Being a God of order and not of chaos, He first came to be with the men of Israel.

The following are a few major provisions of His miraculous life, frozen in time for us all to remember. They are symbolic of His work and life, because He walked the earth as the only God-Man of human history. Look up the verses and summarize each miracle in a sentence:

John 2:1-11: _____

Mark 4:35-41: _____

John 9:1-7: _____

John 4:7-15: _____

Matthew 14:13-21: _____

Mark 1:21-28: _____

Mark 5:21-43: _____

The fact that He was able to perform these miracles is one thing to ponder and marvel about. However, notice that although these are actual historic events, they are also symbolic of a large darkness that had enveloped Israel. In fact, this darkness was worldwide and it was so intense that His people did not receive Him.

In Matthew 12, the religious leaders finally rejected Yeshua and accredited His miracles as being the work of Satan. They called Him Beelzebub, "lord of the flies." This rejection of the Son of God was an unpardonable sin against the power that worked through Him—the Holy Spirit. Their rejection was detrimental, as the people of Israel followed the religious leaders like sheep into a devastating future. It was then that Yeshua began speaking in parables to the people. He continued speaking to them in parables until the end of His life of earth. His ministry, too, became transformed: He was no longer a prophet but the Priest of the world. He knew all along that He would someday be His own sacrifice for all who put their trust in Him alone for salvation. As priest, His duty was to sacrifice, and sacrifice He did! **He** became the Lamb of God, God's only human sacrifice for all of mankind's sin. That is huge! That singular event stands by itself in all the annals of time! God sacrificed a human being, instead of an animal, on our behalf!

For it is impossible that the blood of bulls and goats should take away sins. (Hebrews 10:4, ASV)

In Old Testament days, sacrifices were made daily by the Jews for forgiveness of their sins. When Yeshua, the Lamb of God, shed His blood on the cross, there was no need to do that anymore.

No mere human can ever pay for all the sins of humanity. Understand that only God can offset your and my salvation. During His six agonizing hours on the tree of crucifixion, He paid for the entire sin in our world. This was both retrospective for Old Testament saints and prospective for New Testament saints, you and me. To have that death count for you and me, we must ask Him to be the cover of our sin. Otherwise, it does not include us.

> In all of human history, there has never been another set of six hours during which payment was made to God through the blood of His Son—nor will there ever be!

Today, many people do not know that! They also may not know that if Yeshua had not died on the cross at that precise moment in time as God's only human sacrifice, Abraham, Isaac, Jacob, Job, Jonah, Esther, Ruth, and everyone else, including you and me, would still be in sin, regardless of the amount of good deeds we have done.

> *For the life of the flesh is in the blood, and I have given it for you on the altar to make atonement for your souls, for it is the blood that makes atonement by the life.* (Leviticus 17:11, ESV)

This verse cements together all Scripture, not just some of it. Sin originated with Adam and Eve in the Garden of Eden and exists to (and beyond) this very day. It will be reduced after the Second Coming of Yeshua, but even during the Millennium when Yeshua reigns on earth, and the evil one is in chains, there will still be sin. This is because the sin nature is in the heart of man and not caused by the devil. Only when God does away with the universe, as we know it, and calls down the New Jerusalem will the world be free of the presence of sin.

To review: Yeshua's death removed the **penalty** of sin for the ones who believe in Him. The Holy Spirit, who came into our lives at salvation, offers to take away the **power** of sin from our lives. Finally, the future heaven and earth will forever remove us from the **presence** of sin.

The Leviticus verse is a good one to memorize. It is at the very core of all Scripture. Without shed blood, it is impossible to satisfy the wrath of God toward sin. He installed the sacrificial system, and when people performed the blood sacrifices, it meant they *accepted* that they had been born with a sin nature. The blood of animals was a constant reminder that only God would ever be able to blot out our sin. Without the blood of Yeshua, a person will remain in a state of sin, even if he is good in the world's view. No person born of another human lacks sin in his life, except Yeshua.

For it is impossible for the blood of bulls and goats to take away sins. (Hebrews 10:4, ESV)

Thus, the blood of animals buys nothing permanent for anyone. Neither does any other process bring us salvation: Bible study, good works, religious books, or attending church do not accomplish salvation. Although these are good things, they do not provide what we need most.

The Jewish Passover feast with its original Paschal lamb is a reminder that only God's provision will free us from sin. One can easily see Yeshua's only sacrifice for the sin of mankind in this feast.

Here is another point to consider. Sometimes, good men die for others—as in war. What makes Yeshua's death different? The answer: At His death, He *became* separated from God for the first time in His life. See, we were born separated from God, so that state may seem natural to us. We are familiar with that condition. He was not! During Yeshua's final three hours hanging on the cross, He was God's perfect sacrifice for all humanity. God directed His entire wrath away from us and aimed it on His Son. That thunderbolt killed Him. The answer to the age-old question, "Who killed Jesus?" is, **"You and I did!"** Our sin killed Him. The Romans and the Jews were the *means*; our sin was the *cause*!

Note that Yeshua's divine nature did not "disappear" at the tree. Being the Son of God, He could have stopped His Father's deadly hand at any time. He could have done it at any moment of that six-hour process. Yet for the first time in His life on earth, Yeshua became totally separated from the Father and the Holy Spirit. They were well pleased to put Him to death if He would offer Himself as a guilt offering for others. The exact savagery of those six hours of sacrifice are a mystery to us. We do not know exactly *how* God's requirement for justice was satisfied; we only know that all God was owed for our sin *was* satisfied. That, friends, is the *Gospel*!

On the cross, Yeshua cried out, "My God, my God, why have you forsaken me?" He pleaded, "Let this cup pass from me" to the Father the evening before His death. Then, at the end of His life, He whispered through parched lips, "It is finished." Because of these words, songs have been sung, movies and books written, sermons have been preached to explain what He meant. Of course, the sermons vary. Many people say He was merely a well-intentioned man living an exemplary life. However, the actual story, the Bible account, tells us that He died to substitute Himself for us; He was a guilt offering for every sinner. The God-Man of human history was bound to an altar on Calvary Hill for something He did not do.

He took the full brunt of God's wrath against sin upon Himself. He died for every person who ever lived or would ever live, people to whom punishment for sin was due. That is the real story of the cross of Yeshua! For that reason, if we say the cross was not God's **only** solution for all sin, His anger becomes directed toward us.

Think about that!

After Yeshua died on Calvary, some of His followers quietly removed His body. They carried it into a cave and wrapped it in swaddling clothes. Romans soldiers sealed the entrance to the cave with a large rock, one so heavy that several men could not move it. He, the Cornerstone of all godliness, was sealed in death by a giant stone. The stone at the opening to His tomb became a grim reminder that no person could go inside the cave to be with Him in death. Roman guards were stationed at the front of the tomb to prevent a throng of people from rolling the stone aside.

After three days, a disciple arrived and saw that the boulder had been rolled away from the opening of the cave. It weighed many thousand pounds. Angels had removed the stone from the cave opening, allowing entrance or exit for anyone. Inside the cave, one could clearly see that His body was *absent*. It had vanished! The tomb was empty except for two burial garments that were His wrappings.

Upon the historical certainty of His physical resurrection rests the entire claim of New Testament faith. Biblical faith stands or falls by the single certainty of His resurrection. If He did not return to life, then there is no such thing as salvation from our sin. If He did not rise from death into life, we will bear the penalty for our own sins.

However, He does live!

The reality of His bodily resurrection has always been a reason for celebration by believers in Yeshua. Because He lives, we will continue to celebrate His birth, His life, and His death. What believers in Yeshua also celebrate is God's forgiveness of our sins. That is an important point. He died, but His death on the cross brought freedom to all believers, freedom from eternal death.

It would not have been difficult to quash the story of His crucifixion. The fact that it is a true story provided it a life of its own. When one thinks of Yeshua's death, there are four possible explanations. Only one can be true:

1. He is God. Thus, He is our Savior.
2. He was not telling the truth, so He is a liar; the men who followed Him gave similar false charges and are also liars.
3. He was crazy, a deranged lunatic. Thus, He died in His craziness.
4. The story of Yeshua is a fabrication of history.

In the early 20th century, Albert Henry Ross, a British advertising agent and freelance writer, was tired of the story of Yeshua. As an agnostic and lover of the sciences, he felt it could merely be a revision of historical facts. Therefore, he traveled to Israel to disprove the resurrection. In his book *Who Moved the Stone*, he explains what he tried to prove: "When, as a very young man, I first began seriously to study the life of Christ, I did so with a very definite feeling that, if I may so put it, his history rested on very insecure foundations."[3] During his time in Israel, he used his investigative skills to disprove the gospel accounts of the resurrection. Soon he realized that there is no more important

---

[3] Alfred Henry Ross wrote this book under the pseudonym Frank Morison. The quote here is taken from *Who Moved the Stone?* Grand Rapids, MI: Zondervan, 1956, pg. 9.

person in all of history than Yeshua. In His Name, wars have been fought, pilgrimages organized, and cathedrals built. If His life is a fabrication, then there is no actual basis for most of western civilization. Over the last two millennia, His life story filled the hearts of men with both praise and hateful rejection. From simple homes to the great cathedrals of this world, His Word spread, and no one who was ever confronted with His message could ever stay unfazed. If making an impact on the world makes a person important, then Yeshua is indeed by far the most important person who ever lived. Still, today, people continue to debate the meaning of His life and His death.

The significance of Yeshua is not hard to understand: He is the Lamb of God, who died to pay the full sin debt for you and me, one we were never able to pay for ourselves.

There are several alternative explanations to the fact that His death paid our sin in full. Here are a few examples:

1. **He only swooned on the cross but did not die.** This explanation is contrary to the testimonies of the four individual Gospel accounts of His life and death. If He only swooned, it would contradict each of the four Gospel writers.
2. **His body was taken away by Roman soldiers.** This too cannot be true, because soldiers who were stationed at a tomb were executed if the corpse was stolen or if they fell asleep. Some historian would have reported the death of the ones who watched the body of the Messiah.
3. **His body was removed and hidden by the Jewish religious leaders of the day.** This explanation crumbles if one considers the following: After Yeshua's resurrection and ascension to Heaven, the apostles proclaimed the good news

of salvation for all who believe in the substitutionary death of Messiah. To silence these people forever, the religious leaders merely had to produce the body to contradict the apostolic claims.

4. **His body was stolen by His disciples.** These men were initially scattered and very fearful for their lives when He died. Shortly after His death, they were heartened and began to make provocative statements, which endangered their lives. The only explanation for their bravery is the fact that they did indeed see the risen Messiah.

Yeshua appeared to over 500 men—women and children not included—as proof that He had died and returned to life, according to biblical forecast. These people saw Him, some touched Him, and all believed Him. For example, Peter's life changed dramatically after Yeshua's resurrection, so much so, that he was no longer fearful and headstrong as he was prior to the Messiah's death. Instead, he became more radical about Yeshua. Peter was prepared to die for that truth.

Others, too, became convinced about the truth of His divine nature. Here is what Thomas saw of the resurrected Yeshua:

Then he said to Thomas, "Put your finger here, and see my hands; and put out your hand, and place it in my side. Do not disbelieve, but believe." (John 20:27, ESV)

See my hands and my feet, that it is I myself. Touch me, and see. For a spirit does not have flesh and bones as you see that I have." (Luke 24:39, ESV)

That which was from the beginning, which we have heard, which we have seen with our eyes, which we looked upon and have touched with our hands, concerning the word of life— (1 John 1:1, ESV)

At the conclusion of his investigation, Alfred Henry Ross was no longer an agnostic. Yeshua's incredible life, death, burial, and especially His resurrection convinced him, and he became an outspoken adherent to Yeshua, the God-Man.

Yeshua's finished work on the tree provides an important God principle, one that saved you and me: **vicarious atonement**. Do not allow those two words to become an obstacle in your life. An easy way to remember vicarious atonement is that by it, something *innocent* (Yeshua) pays off the full debt for something else that is *guilty* (you and me). Another way to express this is **imputation**, an old accounting term. Studying Yeshua's unique life, you will see the principle of vicarious atonement continuously repeated. At His death, He paid in full our lifetime of debt to God! He was not just a good man, though He was certainly that too, but He died, bearing a penalty that was due us. Because He was fully man, His death was painful, overwhelming. Because He was God, the separation from His Father was dreadful, but His death fully satisfied the entire wrath of God. No mere man would or could pull that off. Only God can die for others if He chooses!

Things to think about

Is Yeshua the only God-Man of human history? If you think you might know of another, who is it? Remember, Satan can disguise himself as an angel of light to deceive many (2 Corinthians 11:14), and he constantly does that. You will remain conflicted until you come to personally know Yeshua, not just know about Him. He offers the gift of salvation to you if you will receive it, but only if, in genuine repentance, you *believe* on His name.

Are you able to find Yeshua in both the Old and New Testaments? If this is difficult for you, you will probably not be able to understand the major **emphasis** of the Bible. In that event, let someone who does know that truth help you come to know Yeshua.

Do you **trust** Yeshua with your life? Do you trust Him with your death? If not, you have a "belief problem," or you may be a believer who struggles with his faith. Most of us struggle with faith from time to time. The stranglehold of the desires of this world—such things as personal success, money, or possessions—interfere with our spiritual growth. Many believers have a control problem, trying to hold on to whatever they have authority over in a world that constantly challenges our limits. However, faith in God is a valuable benefit to each of us. It does not rust, is not stolen, and cannot be taken away.

> *Do not store up for yourselves treasures on earth, where moth and rust destroy, and where thieves break in and steal.* (Matthew 6:19, NASB)

Please ask someone grounded to help you if you have any doubts. We are all a little afraid of the unknown, so sometimes it is natural to have questions. It is normal for a person to be apprehensive about believing in someone he has never seen or touched.

Again, the wind is a good example for us. We cannot see it, but we experience its force. So, too, is the nature of God! He said, "The righteous shall live by faith," not by sight (Galatians 3:11)! Still, everyone who has trusted Yeshua with His salvation remains certain of His existence, the significance of His shed blood. If you are uncertain about why the blood He shed for you was necessary or if it was sufficient, you should read and reread the Gospel accounts of His matchless life. That is the only way to get real answers about Yeshua.

Read the verses below and fill in the blanks:

¹³ When Jesus came to the region of Caesarea Philippi, he asked his disciples, "Who do people say the Son of Man is?"

¹⁴ They replied, "Some say _____; others say Elijah; and still others, Jeremiah or one of the prophets."

¹⁵ "But what about you?" he asked. "Who do you say I am?"

¹⁶ Simon Peter answered, "You are the Christ, _____ _____." (Matthew 16:13-16, NIV)

Who do you say who Yeshua is? It is time for you to find out!

Seven Steps to a Firm Foundation in Yeshua

Step 4

Sin

The reason we are all struggling is sin. The Bible uses the word "sin" both in the singular and in the plural. Sins in the plural are the result of sin in the singular and not the cause of it. The doctrine of sin continues to create great confusion among many people. They do not like to consider themselves as sinners or in need of a Savior.

We are all in great trouble because of our sin against God. Our sins (such as adultery, deceit, sexual misdeeds, greed, control, etc.) are symptoms of a much bigger sin: that of being separated from the God of Creation. In reality, every sin before salvation is actually the result of that separation from God. After salvation, it is the result of our corrupt cores. Before our salvation, our mistake was our disconnection from Him who came to give us eternal life. Why are we disconnected from Him? Because we prefer to be the gods of our own lives? Yes, of our own lives!

Whether we choose an ascetic life somewhere alone in a cave, living in self-denial, or whether we prefer lives of privilege and abundance somewhere in the Caribbean waters, when we take charge of our own lives, make our own decisions by excluding God, we are telling Him not to bother us. Like wayward children, we do not want to be controlled by anyone, even God. If you doubt you are much the product of your own self-absorption, just let someone awaken you at two in the morning or hide your food or accidentally open your mail and you will discover that you are not as agreeable as you may think yourself to be.

The word "sin" is derived from a Hebrew archery term which literally means "to miss a bull's-eye," "to miss the target (the intended mark)." If you aim at the moon but have a small error of, say, one degree, you will not land on the moon. You will miss it by thousands of miles. Error increases with distance. Over a lifetime, if you are wrong on a little thing, you will find yourself wrong about bigger matters. Our triple adversaries—the world, the flesh, and the devil—continue to deceive us, even when we sleep.

Our biggest enemy in life is our own self. We each possess a deadly core that can only bring us destruction, even when we sleep. It is sin that causes us to stumble and gets us into trouble, and it does that despite us wanting to do what appears very right to us.

For example, consider the fictitious character Robert Miller in the movie "Arbitrage." Miller has lots of money, influence, possessions, friendship, and ladies, yet he keeps rolling the dice of life to own more stuff to which he is not entitled. He can never be satisfied with what he gathers; rather, he also covets what others own—a fitting picture of the sinfulness that surrounds each of us every day. For some people, the pull of ownership is greater, but the truth be known, everyone wants certain possessions of others to which they are not entitled. Can you recall the commandment about not coveting? We all covet much more than we realize. Still, not everyone seems to have a struggle with money or possessions. For example, people with life limiting diseases may be more accommodating to the idea of God. However, just because we see someone open to the Gospel does not mean sin is not present in him. After the crisis passed, just watch how quickly a person returns to a selfish life.

We all want to control our destinies. It is desiring unbridled control of both ourselves and others that gets us into trouble. When we are honest with ourselves, we may understand and accept that we really have very little actual control over anything. Only in the case of suicide can we predict the exact moment of death. We do not know the time or circumstance of our eventual demise, and sometimes, even death by suicide is not assured.

Sin is alive in each of us. It is much more a part of our being than we know. Sinful thinking and sinful acts are so common to us that we cannot much distinguish between actual sin and accidental mistakes. God will not abandon us to such a miserable existence in which we are acting wretchedly, flailing away at fleeting life and grasping for things we are not entitled to hold. God wants us to **realistically** assess who we actually are. He also wants us to know who we are not. For some, it can be a shocking thing to learn who they are not! God is not going to allow us to hold on to our volatile fantasies.

Consider such diversions as alcohol, which is always a fitting subject for dispute. Does it not make sense to blame "spirits" for our aberrant behavior, rather than just say the alcohol released our inhibitions, in reality showing who we really are? People may drink to "loosen up," but alcohol can also be an excuse for us to do things we know we should not do, and then blame the alcohol for that behavior. Sin has many forms! It loves to deceive us!

In Genesis 2:16-17, we read the account of how sin entered the human sphere:

> *[16] The Lord God commanded the man, saying, "From any tree of the garden you may eat freely; [17] but from the tree of the knowledge of good and evil you shall not eat, for in the day that you eat from it you will surely die."* (NASB)

The plot thickens in Genesis 3:1:

> *Now the serpent was more crafty than any beast of the field which the Lord God had made. And he said to the woman, "Indeed, has God said, 'You shall not eat from any tree of the garden'?"* (NASB)

Satan, disguised as a serpent, caused Adam and Eve to doubt God by asking the question, *Indeed, has God said?* Doubt crept in, because Satan, in his craftiness, combined a lie with some truth. They both ate the forbidden fruit, Eve first, and then Adam who was with her in the garden. God punished Adam more severely for disobedience to His Word because of his expected leadership. Being the federal and seminal head of the human race, Adam was held responsible for both his good and bad decisions. God also punished Eve for her deception. She began the first rebellion by manipulating her husband. Thus, Adam rebelled against God being his Creator. We are still doing this today.

God punished both Adam and Eve in multiple ways. The one that affects us the most to this day is their spiritual death. Their rebellion separated them from God. Satan was right in that they did not immediately die physically. What he did not mention, though, is the fact that they would immediately die spiritually. As result of their dead spirit, their souls, that is their will, intellect, and emotions (minds), became corrupted and underwent slow decay. Finally, after hundreds of years, with dead spirits and dead souls, ultimately their bodies died. Adam continued to live for greater than 900 years until he finally died physically. During the days of the first people on earth, hundreds of years were considered a normal lifetime. Today, life is limited to 70, and if in good health, 80 years (Psalm 90).

When a person repents and asks Yeshua to remove the penalty of his sin, his spirit immediately springs to life. With a living spirit, his soul progressively begins to live. Finally, his body will stand erect from the grave! This process is the **reverse** of Adam and Eve's experience in the Garden of Eden. This is what *being born again* means. Being born again of spirit and soul, the body, too, will live in resurrection. That is what is meant by salvation!

Have you been born again?

Consider the fantasy drama, "The Curious Case of Benjamin Buttons," the story of a man who starts aging backwards with some bizarre consequences. This movie has some parallels in our spiritual **reality**. After Yeshua removes the deceitfulness of sin from our hearts, after He circumcises our hearts, we really become alive for the first time.

[28] For he is not a Jew who is one outwardly, nor is circumcision that which is outward in the flesh. [29] But he is a Jew who is one inwardly; and circumcision is that which is of the heart, by the Spirit, not by the letter; and his praise is not from men, but from God. (Romans 2:28-29, NASB)

Without a figurative heart circumcision, we are all dead men walking! You, too, have been entangled by the deceitfulness of sin, much more than you may know! Only God is able to remove sin from you. He will not remove your sin unless you authentically ask Him to be your Savior. You must be honest with Him. Now is a good time for you to know: God loves you. See for yourself in 1 John 4:7:

> *Beloved, let us love one another, for love is from God; and everyone who loves is born of God and knows God.* (NASB)

All people sin and fall short of God's glory. Look up Romans 3:23 and write it down in your own words:

_____
_____
_____

Yeshua Ha-Mashiach was nailed to a tree as the Lamb of God, paying in full for the sins of you and me, in the place of what you and I deserve.

> *When they came to the place called The Skull, there they crucified Him and the criminals, one on the right and the other on the left.* (Luke 23:33, NASB)

> *And Jesus, crying out with a loud voice, said, "Father, into Your hands I commit My spirit." Having said this, He breathed His last.* (Luke 23:46, NASB)

To have His death count for you, you must **receive** Him:

> *But to all who did receive him, who believed in his name, he gave the right to become children of God,* (John 1:12, ESV)

The word *receive* is powerful and descriptive. Here is one analogy, limited as it may be. Imagine you were separated from your parents by circumstances of war. They stayed in Europe, while you escaped to the United States. You were thought to be an orphan of war. One day, you receive a telegram that says your parents discovered that you had survived the war and that they were coming to see you, arriving in New York in a month. Thirty days later, their ship pulls into the harbor. You spot a man and woman who resemble you standing on the windy bridge of the ship, their eyes eagerly searching for you on the dock. The feeling you would have in your heart would not be, "Well, hello folks." That is not what you would think. Instead, your heart would be screaming as you would shout a warm welcome, and a hearty "YES" would fill your entire body! That same "welcome" is what every person must do when he receives Yeshua as Savior. The response is so simple, most folks will not do it, thinking it to be too easy. Instead, they will approach the God of Creation through other means, often through religion. That will not work. Moreover, **it will never work!** Mere intellectual assent is insufficient, insincere, and can deceive one into thinking he has "found God." No, you must welcome Him, love Him, and trust Him for your salvation.

The Bible calls this *receiving Him*. There is no other way to draw near to God. Some churchmen have tried other ways. Other ways never yield life. Salvation is extended to us solely because of God's grace, His goodness, His kindness, and His forgiveness. Salvation is a gift for the true believer who seeks Yeshua as Savior. Salvation is the only exception in life that nullifies the old saying, "There is no free lunch!"

His blotting out of all our sin is vitally important to us; so important, that to not fully appreciate what He did for us is the same as saying "No" to Him. Because Yeshua's death was so costly to God, us wanting to find another alternative is the same as saying, "Who needs you?"

The story is told of a prisoner on death row who is about to be executed by electricity. As the guard walks past his cell, he notices the prisoner furiously flipping through the Bible, turning the pages so quickly that it causes his hair to be windswept.

"I didn't know you were religious, Pete. What are you searching for?" said the smirking guard.

The prisoner answers quietly through a dry mouth, "Loopholes!"

There are no **loopholes** for any of us in life. As a sinner, it will be difficult for you to see your sin for what it is—a **deception**. Things may become more deceptive as you age. We are too **close** to sin to fully appreciate its encompassing hold on us. God never was nor will He ever be accommodating to sin. He does not tolerate any sin. The Bible assures us:

> *The Lord is not slow to fulfill his promise as some count slowness, but is patient toward you, not wishing that any should perish, but that all should reach repentance.* (2 Peter 3:9, ESV)

Here is the important consideration, a backdrop for anyone to experience Yeshua's forgiveness. Repentance! True repentance is a sign that the well of eternal life with God has been primed and that a person is sincere when he asks Yeshua to be his Savior. Yet, without authentic repentance in a person, he is only uttering hollow words, maybe some he has heard in church? Dr. Arnold Fruchtenbaum explains in his book *Faith Alone: The Condition of our Salvation* what biblical repentance is:

> The actual meaning of the Greek word ... is simply "to change one's mind." That is all that biblical repentance means.[4]

Repentance is not simply feeling sorry for one's sins or the attempt to escape from the fiery ordeal that awaits the unbeliever. Repentance means that a person acknowledges the fact that he is a sinner and that the sacrifice of the Son of God alone can save him from the punishment his sinfulness deserves. The change of mind happens when the person looks to God for salvation instead of trying to solve the problem himself. Thus, repentance is a synonym for faith. Only God knows if a person is honest about his belief and wants to be forgiven from his sinful past to move toward new life in Yeshua.

It is time to lay down your arms and receive Messiah Yeshua as your Savior. No one knows the time of his demise. Sudden death has happened to many well-intentioned people over the years. Do you really want to take that chance? Waiting until the last minute is prideful and will probably not work for you. You may never have a better chance to know the salvation God offers than this very day!

Look at the nearly 300-year old lecture preached by Jonathan Edwards (1703-1758) in Enfield, Connecticut, in 1741. This speech titled *Sinners in the Hands of an Angry God* has become an intricate part of the Great Awakening in America (1730-1755). It is considered by some to be the greatest sermon ever preached on American soil, which turned this young country around by its heels

---

[4] Fruchtenbaum, Arnold, *Faith Alone: The Condition of our Salvation*, Ariel Ministries, TX, 2014, p. 91.

and influenced many people to become saved. It even influenced some of the men who later wrote the Constitution of the United States and the Bill of Rights. In his sermon, Edwards brought the issue of sin and salvation to a point when he said, "There is nothing that keeps wicked men at any one moment out of hell, but the mere pleasure of God."

Consider the man who says to himself, "I believe that there is a God in Heaven, just as the Bible says. However, I am not ready to receive Him yet. When I die, I know that God will give me a chance to do whatever it takes to go to His Heaven; I just know it." He is wrong! In addition, he is arrogant! This attitude is one proof that all of us are sinners. Sin tempts us to be our own gods, to choose for ourselves what is morally right or what is morally wrong. However, we do not determine salvation.

Most people want to know with certainty that they are saved. Strangely, few people actually want to change their ways. You may discover that you have been following the deceits of a corrupted worldview, rather than knowing God as He actually is. At this moment, if you know without doubt that you are really saved, please take the time to thank Him for loving you and for blotting out your sin by the blood of His Lamb. If you are not saved, sincerely believe the Gospel message, and if you are sincere, He will save you in an instant. The condition is that you genuinely believe the Gospel message of the Son of God dying on the cross to pay for your sin. **It is the most important thing you will ever do in life!**

Things to think about

To really understand man's biggest problem, one should study what the Bible says about sin. Please read Isaiah 53:6, James 4:17, and 1 John 3:4 and define in your own terms what sin is.

_____

What is the origin of sin according to Isaiah 14:12-14 and Ezekiel 28:15-17?

_____

How would you describe God's position toward sin? (Hab. 1:13)

_____

In the Old Testament, what payment does God require for sin? (Ez. 18:20)

_____

According to the New Testament, did this change? (Rom. 6:23)

_____

The King of the universe, the Creator of all time and circumstance, longs for a **personal relationship** with you even though He knows you through and through. How can you say "No" to that?

Do you feel you have sinned?

_____
_____

If the answer is "No," then why is that?

_____
_____

If you are a believer, but estranged from God, now is the time to return to Him. If you are not a believer, then lay down your weapons of resistance and ask Him to be your God, through Yeshua, the Savior. If you are sincere, He will save you today! If He does not do that, you are not sincere. He knows the difference!

Ask the God of all creation for His gift of salvation. Ask in spirit and truth. If you are sincere, you will find that He will move into your life faster than the speed of light!

Step 5

Justification and Sanctification– the Confusion of it All

Probably, one of the most confusing doctrines in the life of the believer is the distinction between justification and sanctification. Watching the resulting turmoil from many who profess to know these things is like giving a second grader an advanced book about quantum physics. When properly studied, these two doctrines should not really be confusing. Here is an attempt to explain them and provide some clarification for you:

At the moment of salvation, a saved person will become justified in Messiah.

> Justification is
> what Messiah did for us.

Simultaneously, the saved person is sanctified.

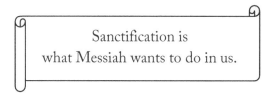

Sanctification is what Messiah wants to do in us.

A believer does not receive only one of these two blessings. Rather, he will receive both of these gifts at the precise moment of his salvation. These twin gifts never fail to exist in the heart of a believer in Yeshua, nor is there a later act of receiving the Holy Spirit, as some may claim, for that would be a second act of grace from God.

Let us review what Yeshua did **for us** with **justification**:
- ✡ He provided us eternal salvation.
- ✡ He provided us His Holy Spirit who forever dwells inside us.
- ✡ He provided us a new way of thinking.
- ✡ He provided us a one-way ticket to eternal existence.

Here are some characteristics of justification:
- ✡ We cannot lose it.
- ✡ We cannot improve it.
- ✡ It is received through faith alone.
- ✡ It lasts forever. Justification does not lessen, despite our mistakes in life.

Did it become evident to you that justification describes our permanent **position** in Yeshua?

Now let us look at what Yeshua wants to do in us with **sanctification**. It is conditional. Conditional means, "If we do x, God will do y." Sanctification is conditioned on our daily walk. Sometimes sanctification manifests itself strongly in us, while other times it may be weaker, even absent.

- ✡ We receive new desires.
- ✡ The Bible begins to be understood much better by us.
- ✡ Scripture reading becomes a pleasure rather than a duty.
- ✡ We will love to share information about God with family and friends.
- ✡ We will begin to have an eternal, rather than temporal perspective about life.

Characteristics of sanctification:

- ✡ We can lose it.
- ✡ We can improve it.
- ✡ It is only apprehended by faith.
- ✡ It is our daily walk.

Notice that there is a continuous, ongoing war against the **flesh** coming from our sanctified lives; there is none coming from our justified lives. During that war, it may feel as if neither justification nor sanctification are existent, even though we know we have been saved. Know that both conditions are always present within us, whether or not we are aware of it.

Our willful disobedience to God feeds our fleshly desires. The sanctification process is empowered by our obedience to God. Therefore, it can be dependent on our circumstances and attitudes. Our justification, on the other hand, never changes. Because Yeshua justified us, we are forever justified. Making mistakes does not negate the permanent position we have in Yeshua, even when we are sometimes unfaithful to Him.

The result of justification in Yeshua is that you will spend eternity with God. The result of sanctification is that you will someday reign with Him (of course, in lesser ways) and be rewarded by Him for faithful living. We do not know exactly what faithfulness will be rewarded by God. For example, some faithfulness may not be genuine. However, whatever He declares to be righteous acts and evidence of our faithfulness, He will reward. He even rewards us some in this life! Look at your circumstances. Though they may be humble, still, if you are faithful, He inflates your life with good things. Being faithful reveals our actual intentions. The fact that some people may be saved, yet live lives in bondage to sin, is another proof of our sinful natures. It ought not to be that way.

Summarily, the justification circle may be best reduced to one word: when a person comes to have a real relationship with the Lord, he has a change of **conscience**. Everyone is born with a conscience, for a conscience is freely given to us by God at birth and distinguishes us from the animal kingdom. In their conscience, some people may be very good, while others may be very bad. However, because a person has a good or bad conscience does not mean they came to know Yeshua at some point, which led to a **changed conscience**. The conscience is where the Holy Spirit does most of His changing work in the life of a believer. Just because a person may go to church, read the Bible, do good works, or talk about Yeshua or the Holy Spirit does not necessarily mean he has a new, a changed conscience. A changed conscience in a person is the real proof that Yeshua lives inside him and will never leave him.

> *[14] For when Gentiles who do not have the Law do instinctively the things of the Law, these, not having the Law, are a law to themselves, [15] in that they show the work of the Law written in their hearts, their conscience bearing witness and their thoughts alternately accusing or else defending them, [16] on the day when, according to my gospel, God will judge the secrets of men through Christ Jesus.* (Romans 2:14-18, NASB)
>
> *I am speaking the truth in Christ—I am not lying; my conscience bears me witness in the Holy Spirit—* (Romans 9:1, ESV)

What we study influences what we believe. For example, if one studies only the Book of Romans in the NT, he may be more likely to embrace certain doctrines that focus on justification. He may do this so much so that he becomes arrogant about his salvation, which in turn leads to **complacency**. Several denominations of Christianity emphasize a positional doctrine to the exclusion of other doctrines. This attitude may be rooted in spiritual pride.

In the same way, if one studies only the Book of James, he is likely to be more **phobic** about his faith. He might strive in his own strength to try and make himself good enough for God. This, too, is spiritual pride.

The truth of the matter is one must have a balanced understanding of both of these doctrines. Sometimes, walking a balanced life can be like a tightrope experience, but the believer must learn to rest in that tension.

Large denominations have been formed on these "over-balances," leading some to conclude that there is a church for anything someone is determined to believe, whether or not that belief is in the Bible. The doctrines mentioned above are apparently different, though both are very much in the plan of God. You can see how confusing it can get. In this present age when churches often eagerly contend for noses, numbers, and nickels, this is a more prevalent problem than in the past. Just know that some believers are complacent in their theology, while some are more phobic in theirs. It ought not to be that way!

Read 2 Timothy 2:3-6. As you read this passage of Scripture, notice that two of the verses speak about our position in Yeshua, while two of the verses speak about our condition in Him. Then, use that method to study other passages of Scripture. You should discover that the Bible addresses both doctrines.

For practice, let us look at another Scripture, Galatians 5:16, which says, *But I say, walk by the Spirit, and you will not carry out the desire of the flesh* (NASB). Is this verse positional or conditional? The answer: conditional. It means, if one walks by the Spirit of God, he will not carry out the desires of the flesh. Again, think: "If I x, then God y," and you will understand it. Otherwise, it does not make much sense.

Let us look at 2 Timothy 2:11-13:

[11] *It is a trustworthy statement:*
For if we died with Him, we will also live with Him;
[12] *If we endure, we will also reign with Him;*
If we deny Him, He also will deny us;
[13] *If we are faithless, He remains faithful, for He cannot deny Himself.*
(NASB)

Can you tell which statements pertain to our position and which to our condition? In reading Scripture, a balanced understanding of "position" and "condition" will help you more clearly understand the flow of what the Bible is saying.

Use that method on other verses. With proper understanding, you will soon be able to differentiate between what Yeshua did for us, and what He wants to do in us. It takes some maturity to overcome any preconceived ideas.

Things to think about

Please read Romans 4:4-5, 5:1, Galatians 2:16, and 3:11. In your own words, describe the relation between grace and justification.

_____
_____
_____

Now look at James 2:14-24. What is the relation between works and justification?

_____
_____
_____
_____

While justification is a one-time event, sanctification is a lifelong, dynamic process. To sanctify means "to set apart." As believers, we are being set apart **from** the sinful influences of this life and **for** the holy plans of God. While we experience sanctification as process, in regards to our position in Yeshua, God has a different view. Read Acts 20:32, 1 Corinthians 6:11, Hebrews 10:10, and Jude 1 and try to describe in your own words how God views our position.

_____
_____

_____
_____
_____

Living life by the Spirit of God can be difficult at times. Some people have compared it to dwelling on a mountain. Every believer is on the mountain. A few make it up to base camp but are too tired to go further and spend their lives getting comfortable at the camp. A smaller few rest, then head for the summit of the mountain. As a believer, you, too, are somewhere on that mountain. Will you be satisfied to just be on the mountain, or will you climb up to base camp, maybe even to the summit? What you do with your salvation, how you live life after salvation, is your choice. Prayer by other believers might influence your choice, but if you live life in a waste, you will certainly not make it to the summit.

Look up 1 Corinthians 3:10-15 and fill in the blanks. The version used here is the ESV.

> [10] According to the grace of God given to me, like a skilled master builder I laid a _____, and someone else is building upon it. Let each one take care how he builds upon it. [11] For no one can lay a foundation other than that which is laid, which is Jesus Christ. [12] Now if anyone _____ on the foundation with gold, silver, precious stones, wood, hay, straw— [13] each one's work will become manifest, for the Day will disclose it, because it will be revealed by _____, and the fire will test what sort of _____ each one has done. [14] If the work that anyone has built on the foundation survives, he will receive a _____. [15] If anyone's work is burned up, he will suffer loss, though he himself will be saved, but only as through fire.

Does this passage mostly speak about condition or position?

Now, look up Galatians 3:8 and fill in the blank:

And the Scripture, _____ that God would justify the Gentiles by faith, preached the gospel beforehand to Abraham, saying, "In you shall all the nations be blessed." (ESV)

The last verse to look at in this context is 2 Thessalonians 2:13:

But we ought always to give thanks to God for you, brothers beloved by the Lord, because God _____ you as the firstfruits to be saved, through sanctification by the Spirit and belief in the truth. (ESV)

Step 6

Living in the Power of the Holy Spirit

---

[16] But I say, walk by the Spirit, and you will not gratify the desires of the flesh. [17] For the desires of the flesh are against the Spirit, and the desires of the Spirit are against the flesh, for these are opposed to each other, to keep you from doing the things you want to do. [18] But if you are led by the Spirit, you are not under the law. (Galatians 5:16-18, ESV)

As a believer, this may be one of the most **important** principles you you can live by. There are two misconceptions about the Holy Spirit of God. At first, these errors may seem diametrically opposed to one another, but they are actually similar. They both miss the mark and lead believers down difficult paths they do not have to traverse.

One error is to view the Holy Spirit as a means to **having an experience**. That experience usually becomes a platform for a person's life. It leads a person to the mistaken conclusion that he must pray for specific miracles to happen in his life, in order to enable him to feel closer to Yeshua. People who are following this thought process tend to "speak in tongues." They prophesy or find and follow a presumed prophet or prophetess, and often they pray to have a full complement of all the gifts from God. They strive to be more filled with Yeshua.

Unfortunately, this doctrine often leads to an "us versus them" mentality. Judgment sets in, and anyone who does not have a "sign gift," such as tongues or prophecy or healing or whatever, may be considered to be unspiritual at best or unsaved at worst.

In the experience model, all focus is on the gift rather than the Giver, no matter the denial. It promotes an idea called "a second act of grace." The experience becomes an add on to salvation indicating that Yeshua's death on the cross was insufficient to free the believer from the bondage of sin. The error, then, lies in the fact that it is not salvation by faith through grace alone but salvation plus supernatural experience. The person living the experience elevates himself over what Yeshua has accomplished on the cross.

That being said, God does have great experiences for us, some are pretty unbelievable, but they are neither regular, predictable, nor are they bottled up and sold like patent medicine.

> *Beloved, do not believe every spirit, but test the spirits to see whether they are from God, for many false prophets have gone out into the world.* (1 John 4:1, ESV)

A second error is in seeing God's Spirit (some call it His energy) as part of His nature rather than as a **distinct personality**. The Holy Spirit is not merely another attribute of God, but a Person with will, intellect, and emotions. People who believe this error may say that the Trinity is God the Father, God the Son, and the Bible. This is a wrong view of God. The idea dismisses that the Holy Spirit, the third Person of the Trinity, is fully God, who enters every believer at the time of salvation. This Spirit of God wants to transform a believer over time into a more mature being.

> *But the Helper, the Holy Spirit, whom the Father will send in my name, he will teach you all things and bring to your remembrance all that I have said to you.* (John 14:26, ESV)

The point of this error is that it can place a believer into bondage of "religion." We can memorize Scripture as much as we want to, but if we do not understand that it was the Holy Spirit who inspired the authors, we missed the point!

When Yeshua departed from the earth, He promised that all believers, large and small, regardless of their race or nationality, would receive His Helper, the Holy Spirit. The Holy Spirit alone empowers every believer, who is willing to grow, to become more mature in the faith. He alone is the One who works on the sanctification of the believer and transforms him into the image of the Son of God. He always points the way to Yeshua! Furthermore, He promised that the believer will not have to walk by his own efforts but by the One on whom the Son Himself depended.

Thus, there are two errors we need to avoid. The first one is seeing the Holy Spirit as an independent power. The second one is seeing Him as part of the Father's character. Both views are wrong!

Here is a review: the Holy Spirit is a distinct personality. He indwells each believer at the moment of authentic salvation. A believer may not realize it because the early days of salvation can be dizzying! Some, maybe most, believers may have a few experiences from the moment of salvation. They will probably start praying for small things, like finding a convenient parking spot in an overcrowded street and be overjoyed when the prayer is answered, or they might suddenly hear a Bible message that speaks right into their lives. These experiences are common and bring comfort and confirmation for the young believer.

Later as the believer begins to live out a life of faith and not one of sight, these experiences may seem more distant. His growth moves him from milk to meat. Hebrews 5:11-13 explains what we mean:

> *[11] Concerning him we have much to say, and it is hard to explain, since you have become dull of hearing. [12] For though by this time you ought to be teachers, you have need again for someone to teach you the elementary principles of the oracles of God, and you have come to need milk and not solid food. [13] For everyone who partakes only of milk is not accustomed to the word of righteousness, for he is an infant....* (Hebrews 5:11-13, NASB)

Meat—or solid food, as it says here—is not as easy to digest for new believers as milk, and milk is the correct food at the beginning of your walk with Yeshua. The danger is that the believer stays on milk. The various enticements of the world will tempt him to opt for immaturity instead of maturity.

Here is a good principle to remember:

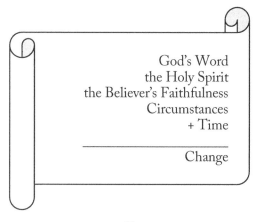

If any step is omitted, what is taking place is probably not real change but a new wrapper.

The Holy Spirit is a real Being, a full member of the Trinity, equal to the Father and the Son. We must resist the temptation to say there is one God with three hats. We also must resist the temptation to worship three different gods as separate beings.

Here are some reasons why the Holy Spirit is fully God:

- The Holy Spirit has will, intellect, and emotions. Like the Father and the Son, He has freedom of choice.
- The Holy Spirit is not just a portion of God's personality; rather, He is a **distinct person**. Yeshua sent Him to His followers so that they would understand the things of God. He is fully God who has a different responsibility than the other two members of the Trinity.

Some believers falsely assume that the Spirit of God will empower them only if they do spiritual things. They may seek to make it happen by asking for specific signs (tongues, prophecies, faith healing) or by memorizing countless Bible verses, going to church three times a week, and teaching Sunday school. Acts of service are fine, but they do not increase the favor with which God is looking upon the person.

In Old Testament times, the Holy Spirit entered and departed from people as He saw fit. One example of this is King Saul. At times, the Holy Spirit clearly guided the man, and at other times, He left him, which usually ended in devastation. After the crucifixion of Yeshua, the Holy Spirit came to live inside every believer. He seals the person at the moment of his salvation (Eph. 1:13). Sadly, many believers live out their days in the futility of their own efforts without the Holy Spirit's influence. Existence can present many struggles for us if we do that.

Exactly what does it mean to "walk by the Spirit?" Every believer has two opposing natures living inside him during his life on earth. One nature has fleshly desires and seeks things to fulfill its own longings. It is what the Bible calls the old sin nature. The other nature is a new spirit within the believer, which is a right understanding of God. These two natures are in continuous opposition to each other.

Our sin nature has one agenda, and our spirit has a different agenda. If we give in to the temptations of our sin nature, they will yield only chaos, even death. If, on the other hand, we live by the Spirit of God, it will lead to wisdom.

Why do believers not have the full benefit of eternal things while on earth? One of the reasons may be that they are not living in the power of the Spirit of God. Some believers mature in spiritual things. They have no guile and are not guided by the temporal things that surround them. Most other believers in Yeshua practice a form of "cultural Christianity." They may attend church, fly to Africa on a mission trip, utter some repetitious blessing before meals, and even pray in times of need. Are they living according to the flesh or by the Spirit of God? Every believer is in either one of these two camps; he is either in the world or in the Spirit.

Nothing forces us to pursue fleshly things. Believing that good things can be acquired by being "religious," we pursue works instead of letting the Holy Spirit guide us. The truth is this: things we acquire in the flesh are temporal. They vanish.

One need not be saddened by various difficulties encountered during this lifetime. Understanding the work of the Holy Spirit can be a slow process, and we make many mistakes. Such is the makeup of all believers. Three steps forward, two steps back. Sometimes, it is two steps forward, three steps back. Or simply, three steps back. Some people make the same mistakes again and again. Unfortunately, many believers never come to a proper understanding of the personal God who lives within them. For such a person, the Holy Spirit may be someone they occasionally hear about in church. Thus, their lives have minimal, if any, power to overcome the great difficulties that lie ahead.

How do you think it would be if a believer were to live out this life in the full power of the Holy Spirit? Such a person would be satisfied, content with life, realizing that God is exactly who He says He is!

> *These are the days of Abraham's life, 175 years. Abraham breathed his last and died at a good old age, and he was an old man and full of his years* (another version says "satisfied") *and was gathered to his people* (Genesis 25:7-8, ESV).

How many believers do you know who are really satisfied with life? Surely not as many as there should be! Many claim to be satisfied, but they are weary, and more so with time, and so they may feign satisfaction.

> *They who wait for the Lord shall renew their strength; they shall mount up with wings like eagles; they shall run and not be weary; they shall walk and not faint.* (Psalm 40:31, ESV)

How many folks do you know who live that way? Did you know that satisfaction is a promise God made to His children? Read the verse again. He promises that those who walk with Him will not grow weary, nor will they faint when they experience the difficulties of life. Remember, when God makes a promise, He **always** keeps it.

The Holy Spirit is waiting to be more dynamic in the life of the believer. He promises wisdom for the godly person, the one who longs for God's provision in his life, the one who completely trusts His promises.

A person who lives by the power of the Holy Spirit will never flutter his wings like a hummingbird in repetitious cycles, but he will soar great distances to the slow cadence of eagle wings. These wings will glide him over mountains, valleys, and water, expending very little energy to stay aloft. He will not tire in whatever trial may come his way.

To walk through life in the power of the Holy Spirit is a **condition**, not a position in Yeshua. In other words, a believer is free to do it or not do it, whichever he chooses. Soaring with the God of the universe is not a phenomenon that occurs later in salvation. If believers choose to walk through life mostly in the power of their own flesh, that is their choice. But much better is the one who learns to walk in the power of the Holy Spirit.

Salvation is meant to be a partnership with God, just as it was with Adam and Eve in the Garden of Eden. Notice that God often let them be alone to experience the results of their own decisions. He was not a puppeteer, pulling their strings first to the right, then to the left. He wanted them to subdue the creation, but waited for them to remember Him in their lives. He continues to do that. He always will.

When a person does not know which direction to turn, it is often a sign of not understanding that God does not want believers to be robots, but will show us the right way when we ask. Sometimes, when we turn in a direction He has not chosen for us, it still works out. Other times, it becomes a mistake. Likewise, when people become imprisoned to the world through wrong choices, it is not His desire for us. Know that wrong choices help the wise to start making right choices.

When we develop a healthy understanding of how to walk under the influence of God, there will always be doubt. Are we doing the right thing? Are we yielding to the guidance of the Spirit enough? Maturity means that we have developed a healthy understanding of His ways. It satisfies the longing of every believer's heart. To walk according to fleshly desires invites trouble and leads to imprisonment, which is never God's intention for us.

So, to partner with God is to walk in the power of the Holy Spirit. We must trust Him in every area of life. When Abraham placed Isaac on an altar, it created a fitting picture of God wanting us to trust Him on the altar of our lives. He does not encourage us in "religious posturing." He expects us to trust Him in every circumstance of life. He expects that we count on His grace and not on our "religion."

People who is have a lot of trust in the world, often smile and express some aphotic cliché of endearment like, "Hi brother," "Blessings to you," and, "Jesus is on the throne!" They may be grasping for some brass ring of life from their plastic ponies. They may love temporal things, but speak spiritual sounding utterances.

To have the right idea of how it is to walk through life in the power of the Holy Spirit, one must, as it is said, "let go and let God." Thinking about it, this should be much easier than trusting in the world we live in. However, letting go of something can be very difficult. It can be a "tar baby."

Things to think about

Level of Commitment:

The following is a stratification that defines believers. The ones on the top walk closely with Yeshua, while the ones at the bottom might not even know Him.

1. Very Important People (VIP);
2. Very Resourceful People (VRP);
3. Very Teachable People (VTP);
4. Very Nice People (VNP, the preponderance of Christianity);
5. Very Draining People (VDP, of which there are more in the world than we would expect to see).

In the first few categories are people who have learned to walk through life in the power of the Holy Spirit. They are the ones who soar on wings like eagles. They have learned to trust God through every circumstance, a little at a time, but they have come to trust Him for being who He says He is.

Which is your category?

_____

Many people think they are a combination of categories, at times one way, at other times another. That is not true for most believers. No one really vacillates much back and forth between two groups.

Decide today, in which of the five groups you want to live. As you do, remember Joshua, who raised his banner long ago, declaring,

> *And if it is evil in your eyes to serve the LORD, choose this day whom you will serve, whether the gods your fathers served in the region beyond the River, or the gods of the Amorites in whose land you dwell. But as for me and my house, we will serve the LORD.* (Joshua 24:15 ESV)

Do you walk in the power of the Holy Spirit and serve God, or do you merely attend church and go on mission trips with friends twice a year?

People who influence our lives:

Every believer should have several people in his life: one or a few Pauls (mature believers), at least one Barnabas (encourager), and a few Timothys (new believers whom they disciple). Whenever we see or read about someone falling from grace, we can be certain that they do not have those kinds of people in their lives.

Do you have a Paul in your life? _____

Do you have a Barnabas in your life? _____

Do you have a Timothy in your life? _____

Step 7
A Balanced Life in Yeshua

Using the groups at the end of lesson 6 should help believers to traverse the sometimes difficult paths of their faith walk. For those who continue to grow in godly wisdom rather than simply being "religious," life works out well. Being a "Very Teachable Person" or a "Very Important Person" is more godly than merely being a "Very Nice Person," although every believer is supposed to be nice, meaning non contentious, even when circumstances are difficult.

We do not want to omit anyone from authentic discipleship, because everyone starts out a "nice person." Many grow into more mature believers. However, you should not be stuck with a "draining person," who not only does not accept responsibility for his circumstances, but then may get mad at you for not fixing them. You should not ignore someone draining, but neither should you commit a lifetime of trying to help them out of the quicksand.

For any believer in Yeshua, a balanced life is essential. The path to authentic spiritual maturity—though it can be rocky at times—is considerably easier than the heavy yoke of "self" that the world tries to hang around our necks. In Matthew 11:29-30, Yeshua, too, spoke about a yoke:

> Take My yoke upon you and learn from Me, for I am gentle and humble in heart, and YOU WILL FIND REST FOR YOUR SOULS. For My yoke is easy and My burden is light. (NASB)

If there is freedom in Yeshua, why is it that He also calls life a yoke?

Living a life in Yeshua is a responsibility. Make no mistake. But that responsibility is much lighter than the heavier responsibility the world requires. **Spiritual maturity** in this life is more important than simply making a **decision** to live a good life, go to church, throw some money in the plate, and maybe teach a Sunday school class. There is nothing wrong with these, but they can be substitutes for authentic maturity. Instead, use the formula in the previous chapter, and you will find yourself undergoing change.

Not being mature at the start of our walks with Yeshua is a function of the myriad of attractions we hold onto in order to stay close to our perception of the world. These attractions are things that seem important to us, but are really not. Are we living our lives more deeply dependent on these passing things than depending on God who created us? To bring us into better alignment with Him, we should **become more mature** in our walks with Yeshua.

All of us are an amalgam of body, soul, and spirit. So at our core, we are **tripartite,** or three-phase, human beings. There may be some confusion about the human heart because the world sees no real distinction between the soul of a man and the spirit of a man. But the Bible separates these two facets when it teaches that our souls contain our wills, our intellects, and our emotions. If our spirits have been renewed and are alive now, they will be in communication with the living God. What does this mean? Before we came to know God, we were spiritually dead. The term "born again" expresses this phenomenon, because at the moment of salvation, the believer's spirit comes to life. This is what Yeshua is referring to when He says to Nicodemus, "You must be born again." Let us read the whole conversation, which is recorded in John 3:

> [1] Now there was a man of the Pharisees, named Nicodemus, a ruler of the Jews; [2] this man came to Jesus by night and said to Him, "Rabbi, we know that You have come from God as a teacher; for no one can do these signs that You do unless God is with him." [3] Jesus answered and said to him, "Truly, truly, I say to you, unless one is born again he cannot see the kingdom of God."
>
> [4] Nicodemus said to Him, "How can a man be born when he is old? He cannot enter a second time into his mother's womb and be born, can he?" [5] Jesus answered, "Truly, truly, I say to you, unless one is born of water and the Spirit he cannot enter into the kingdom of God. [6] That which is born of the flesh is flesh, and that which is born of the Spirit is spirit. [7] Do not be amazed that I said to you, 'You must be born again.' [8] The wind blows where it wishes and you hear the sound of it, but do not know where it comes from and where it is going; so is everyone who is born of the Spirit."
>
> [9] Nicodemus said to Him, "How can these things be?" [10] Jesus answered and said to him, "Are you the teacher of Israel and do not understand these things? [11] Truly, truly, I say to you, we speak of what we know and testify of what we have seen, and you do not accept our testimony. [12] If I told you earthly things and you do not believe, how will you believe if I tell you heavenly things? [13] No one has ascended into heaven, but He who descended from heaven: the Son of Man. [14] As Moses lifted up the serpent in the wilderness, even so must the Son of Man be lifted up; [15] so that whoever believes will in

Him have eternal life. [16] "For God so loved the world, that He gave His only begotten Son, that whoever believes in Him shall not perish, but have eternal life. (NASB)

Every person who ever lived was born with a dead spirit; from the dope pusher to the president of a nation, to the beggar, to the pope— every soul was that way. When a person is saved, his or her spirit immediately comes alive. Thereafter, it will never cease to exist. Even if the born again person opts not to walk in unison with his God, but live life in the flesh, his spirit will not die again. God will never remove salvation from him.

As mentioned before, the tripartite human nature is often misunderstood. In today's culture, the word "spirit" has become a common buzzword. For example, there is a town in the western USA, which promotes living life more fully through a good balance of body, mind, and spirit. It is suggested that you will "feel" better when you get in touch with your "spiritual nature." The spirit of a person is often seen as being equal to the soul. In that context, the people who speak about the spirit within them say that you can get in touch with your intended "personal enlightenment."

That is not the biblical meaning of the spirit of a person. The worldly form of "spirit" is a counterfeit experience and seeks to imitate the reality of a spirit that has been made alive by God. When "spirit" is used in the Bible, it is always meant to convey that a believer in Yeshua has a living spirit where the Spirit of God resides. Realize that the precepts of the world are often in opposition to the Word of the God.

Now may the God of peace Himself sanctify you entirely; and may your spirit and soul and body be preserved complete, without blame at the coming of our Lord Jesus Christ. (1 Thessalonians 5:23, NASB)

And do not fear those who kill the body but cannot kill the soul. Rather fear him who can destroy both soul and body in hell. (Matthew 10:28, ESV)

For just as the body without the spirit is dead, so also faith without works is dead. (James 2:26, NASB)

and the dust returns to the earth as it was, and the spirit returns to God who gave it. (Ecclesiastes 12:7, ESV)

For the word of God is living and active and sharper than any two-edged sword, and piercing as far as the division of soul and spirit, of both joints and marrow, and able to judge the thoughts and intentions of the heart. (Hebrews 4:12, ESV)

Many other verses of Scriptures assure us that the spirit of a man is different from the soul of a man, and both are distinct from the physical body of a man. Here is a reality that can change your thinking in a moment of time: You should know that Yeshua is the only man who from the moment of his birth had a living spirit.

When Adam sinned, his spirit died immediately. In Genesis 2:17, God had warned him, *but from the tree of the knowledge of good and evil you shall not eat, for in the day that you eat from it you will surely die* (NASB). Notice that his body did not die for many years after his spiritual death. However, his spiritual death assured his later physical death. There was no spiritual life left in him, so he died **immediately** in his spirit, although his body lived for many years afterward.

Now, what happened to his soul? Not having a living spirit, Adam's soul (Hebrew: *nephesh*) began to die **progressively**. His thoughts became more corrupted with time, his selfishness grew stronger. Having a dead spirit and a dead soul took his life away; he **ultimately** died physically and went to a dusty end.

Conversely, at the instant of authentic salvation, the spirit of a person **immediately** springs to life. He is said to be **born again**, an appropriate expression. With a living spirit, his soul **progressively** begins to live. Eventually, every believer in Yeshua **ultimately** will arise from his resting place to live in eternity with God.

This process is the exact reverse of Adam's experience. At the moment of salvation, the spirit of the believer begins to live. Thereafter, the soul begins to "think" in a more godly way (notice that not everyone thinks completely godly, all the time, especially immediately after salvation), and finally the body will be resurrected. Remember, even though a person may be born again in spirit, that does not mean they will not make mistakes in life. After all, the sin nature is still very active in the duality of life in which the sin nature and the spirit strive with each other. We do not have to respond to a sinful nature, but the fact is there are times when we do. That is the reason why maturity is so important.

At this point, you may want to stop and think through the process of salvation. Some of these thoughts may be new for you. Where are you on the continuum of maturity? Maturity is a great responsibility for every believer.

To repeat an eternal Bible principle, salvation **justifies** you forever in God's sight. It is fixed and cannot be improved. Justification is dependent on God alone! But that does not assure you of a good existence now. It is like getting a driver's license at age 16, which merely prepares you to learn how to drive.

Sanctification pertains to your walk with Yeshua. How you live your life after you have received Him is dependent on the choices you make. Sanctification is "conditional," and no one is forcing you to mature. If you are not mature, many snares await you. Some of these may seem to benefit you for a season, but they will not last. They cannot last.

Below are some points by which you can test yourself. They will help you to discover if you are a believer. If you are a believer, they will help you discern if you are maturing the way you should.

> *Test yourselves to see if you are in the faith; examine yourselves! Or do you not recognize this about yourselves, that Jesus Christ is in you—unless indeed you fail the test?* (2 Corinthians 13:5, NASB)

Paul clearly admonishes us to test ourselves and to see if we are becoming mature in the faith of Yeshua.

The following are some of the traits we want to mature in:

1. **Always be passionately committed to** Yeshua.
2. **Be personally pure.** This could easily be at the top of the list of "to be-s." By being pure, a believer does not merely pursue religious gymnastics. It means he lives out his life according to the songs we sing in church. The lyrics are not just words; they reflect our trust in Yeshua. Often there is a discrepancy between what we sing about and what we actually do. Appearance and reality do not line up. Being pure means we are becoming more mature, admitting our shortcomings to one another, and not being too fond of our strengths. Over time, our personalities should become more like those of Yeshua, although we will always be short of His ideal nature.
3. **Be biblically measured.** Since the Bible is God-breathed truth, your life should conform to the Scriptures and not to the world. That does not mean you are to be a robot. You should learn to respond to all situations according to biblical principles, which were written for your benefit. By discovering what the Bible has to say on a matter, you should

begin to think more rightly. The Bible should be your handbook, your companion, your "owner's operating" manual for living a good and godly life. Remember, God cares more about **who** you are than **what** you know or profess to know, although knowing good doctrine can influence much (but not all) of who we are.

4. **Be family centered.** Your family should be more important to you than your personal accomplishments. Family care should always precede your job and your church. If you do not properly keep up the garden of your life, how will you manage the things of God? It is not a difficult concept. Many "nice" believers have their priorities inverted, putting church and church activities before family. Doing this is antithetical to how Scripture asks you to live life.

5. **Be evangelistically bold.** There are CEOs of large companies who can present a perfect stock report to savvy shareholders, yet feel uncomfortable talking to a person about their faith in Yeshua. Why is that? We all wear masks. We may not know we are wearing them, or we do not care to know that we are wearing them. A wise pastor once advised, "Do all you can to convince someone that Yeshua Ha'Mashiach is the only begotten Son of God and is the only way to spend the rest of eternity with God, and if necessary, use words!" Every family has its own inherent difficulties in life, but inasmuch as life concerns you, you should live in such a way as to not cause anyone else to reject the claims of Yeshua.

6. **Be socially responsible.** Being socially responsible does not mean we are to lie down in the doorways of abortion clinics, (although, God may encourage some to do that), but we are to think through important issues of the day and have godly

views on social matters. Certain issues of the day, like voter registration, gay marriage, alcohol excess, business, and our pastimes are actually things about which we should be sensible and reasonable, not obsessive. "I don't know" is not the proper response when we feel something to be wrong. We should always consider other people, but not be too abrasive with them. Saying a little in love can be more effective than angry confrontation. It is possible to take a stand with some people while prayerfully seeking to develop relationships with them and others.

We do not mean to imply that sometimes it is not appropriate to withdraw from a friendship, or say hard things to someone, but many disputes are incited by the anger or impatience of a believer.

When someone asks how we view a matter, it should not take much thought to express a godly view, rather than a politically safe word. Thinking through some of those issues will help you be prepared for whatever comes your way in life. Sometimes, we may even change our positions, but at least we should think through the issues of the day from a godly perspective before we speak. We should seek to influence others with what is right and what is wrong. On the other hand, some believers may be too colorful when they talk about such issues as politics, leadership, and abortion. Therefore, their opinions may be only that and not really God's leadership. We want to always influence the lives of others in good ways. That is the way of God.

The points described here will always bring challenges to us. We will face periods of failure. However, the maturation process is dynamic, not static. When we fail, we must strap on our boots again and do what is right, apologizing if necessary. Being properly balanced is a lifelong process, but it will become easier with practice and age.

Another promise we must never forget is that salvation includes our eventual **glorification**. This means that God will ultimately perfect the believer. Turning this into an equation of sorts, this is what we should always keep in mind:

$$\frac{\text{Justification} + \text{Sanctification} + \text{Glorification}}{\text{Salvation}}$$

Contrary to popular legend, glorification does not mean that when we die we ascend to some heavenly stratosphere for the rest of eternity, that we sing in some celestial choir, have a cape, pluck harp strings, wear royal garments, or cover ourselves with white robes. Some of these may happen to an extent, but the main point of salvation is godly behavior, not what we will wear.

It is amazing how little thought many believers have given about what God has promised us for all eternity. They have only a dreamy, ethereal view of the hereafter and live life in that fantasy. The truth is, something much greater than fantasy awaits the believer in Yeshua. We can read this in 1 Corinthians 2:9:

but just as it is written,

"THINGS WHICH EYE HAS NOT SEEN AND EAR HAS NOT HEARD,
AND WHICH HAVE NOT ENTERED THE HEART OF MAN,
ALL THAT GOD HAS PREPARED FOR THOSE WHO LOVE HIM." (NASB)

Encouragement is necessary for every believer, lest he become separated from the flock of other believers! We have not been saved for nothing, but for the reality of spending eternity with the King of kings! God gives authentic salvation to everyone who believes in Yeshua. It is for every believer, every person who has asked Yeshua, "May your blood sacrifice count for me too?" The momentary trials of this life are not equivalent to that certainty.

For I consider that the sufferings of this present time are not worthy to be compared with the glory that is to be revealed to us. (Romans 8:18, NASB)

Things to think about

Just as our physical birth is only the beginning of our life here on earth, being born again of the Spirit is only the beginning of our eternal life. The new birth encompasses many privileges, but it also carries responsibilities. It is therefore important to consider the following questions:

1. Summarize the three elements of our new position:
John 10:10 _____
John 7:38 _____
1 John 5:4 _____

2. After a person has been born again, there are several things that become his responsibility. Look up the verses and summarize which good habits the Bible encourages.

Psalm 1:2, 2 Corinthians 6:14-18

_____

_____

Ecclesiastes 4:9-10, Proverbs 24:6

_____

_____

Romans 10:9, Luke 12:8

_____

_____

_____

3. Summarize 1 Corinthians 6:19-20 in your own words. What do these verses mean to you?

_____

_____

_____

_____

_____

4. The list of things we ought to do is long. One day, you will have to take the time to carefully study the Law of Messiah, which is contained in the New Testament. (It is important to know that the

Law of Messiah and the Law of Moses are distinct. We do not want you to think you have to keep *Torah*!) Please note that keeping the Law of Messiah will not make you more acceptable to God. He has already accepted you when you placed your trust in what Yeshua has done on your behalf. An obedient heart to what Messiah wants us to do will lead to maturity and an "easier" life insofar as He knows what is best for us. Having said this, look up the following verses and jot down how they present keys to a victorious life in Yeshua.

John 14:21 _____

Romans 12:1-2 _____

2 Corinthians 4:5 _____

Ephesians 5:18 _____

Colossians 3:2 _____

Hebrews 11:6 _____

5. We all stumble and make mistakes. Please know that your stumbling does not change your position. Nevertheless, our sins do affect our relationship with the Father and, therefore, need to be dealt with. Look at verse 1 John 1:9 and figure out the different responsibilities. What role does God play in the reestablishing of our relationship with Him after we have sinned, and what is our responsibility?

_____
_____
_____

6. Write down a few things that changed in your life since you became a believer.

_____
_____
_____

Postscript

Congratulations on finishing this basic foundational study of God's Word! These steps are crucial for you to develop a proper understanding of God and to share His matchless material with others.

God's Word is powerful; it is life altering. The Scriptures mentioned in this book should provide you with a wellspring of good information to get you started.

At this point, it should be repeated that you will not get very far in your walk with Yeshua until you become dependent on the Holy Spirit. He is the sole person of the trinity who can help you understand the life and work of Yeshua Ha'Mashiach and who can lead all believers to authentic maturity in Him.

> *But the Helper, the Holy Spirit, whom the Father will send in my name, he will teach you all things and bring to your remembrance all that I have said to you.* (John 14:26, ESV)

Living under the influence of the Holy Spirit cannot be overemphasized. He is God, He is real, and He is waiting for you to ask Him into your life.

You will do well to have another person in your life who is mature in the faith and who will pray for you and be an encouragement to you.

Yossie Meir

About the Author

Dr. Yossie Meir was born into a Jewish home. He studied medicine and became a diagnostician. In 1972, he came to faith in his Messiah Yeshua through the teaching of another Messianic Jew, Dr. Arnold Fruchtenbaum. Mentored by this excellent scholar, Dr. Meir quickly became a teacher himself, equipping many men with the knowledge and understanding of the Scriptures. He and his wife have four children and eight grandchildren. This is his first book.

CPSIA information can be obtained at www.ICGtesting.com
Printed in the USA
LVOW01s1716220515

439255LV00002B/3/P